VALUES OF THE KINGDOM OF GOD

HOW TO DEVELOP A GODLY CHARACTER

DR HENDRIK VORSTER

COMMENT FROM A WORLD LEADER

REV MARGARET COURT AO, MBE

Senior Pastor - Victory Life International - Perth, Australia

"Dr Hendrik Vorster has a great wealth of the Word of God and leadership strategies. He is on Yonggi Cho's Church Growth International Board with me and is a partner with Victory Life International; he is also a valuable teacher on Church Planting to the Nations of the world.

'Values of the Kingdom of God' *is full of golden nuggets to help you build Godly character and lead a successful life by applying each of the Kingdom values to your daily walk.*

This is a valuable tool for your life and maturity."

CONTENTS

Introduction   ix

PART I
1. Spiritual roots   3
2. Values defined   11
3. Maturity comes through Obedience   17

PART II
1. Humility   27
2. Mournfulness   30
3. Meekness   33
4. Spiritual Passion   36
5. Mercifulness   39
6. Purity   42
7. Peacemaker   46
8. Patience   49
9. Example   52
10. Custodian   54
11. Reconciliatory   57
12. Resoluteness   60
13. Loving   63
14. Discreetness   66
15. Forgiving   69
16. Kingdom of God Investor   72
17. God-minded   76
18. Kingdom of God prioritizer   79
19. Introspective   82
20. Persistence   85
21. Consideration   88
22. Conservative   91
23. Fruit-bearing   94
24. Practitioner   97

25. Accountability	100
26. Living by Faith	103
27. Childlikeness	106
28. Unity	109
29. Servanthood	113
30. Loyalty	116
31. Gratefulness	119
32. Stewardship	121
33. Obedience	125
34. Carefulness	128
35. Compassion	131
36. Caring	135
37. Confident	138
38. Steadfastness	141
39. Contentment	144
40. Teachable	147
41. Deference	151
42. Diligence	155
43. Trustworthiness	158
44. Gentleness	161
45. Discernment	164
46. Truthfulness	168
47. Generosity	171
48. Kindness	175
49. Watchfulness	178
50. Perseverance	182
51. Honouring	186
52. Submissive	190
Afterword	195
Notes	197

Values of the Kingdom of God
(How to develop a Godly Character and keep it)

A practical guidebook to develop a Kingdom of God Character

This book explores multiple aspects to developing godly values consistent with Kingdom of God living.

www.churchplantingdoctor.com
resources@churchplantingdoctor.com

Copyright © Churchplantingdoctor.com 2019
All rights reserved.

ISBN 13-978-1-7338266-0-0

No part of this publication may be reproduced, stored in a retrieval system, or transmitted in any form or by any means, electronic, mechanical, photocopying, recording or otherwise, without written permission from Hendrik J. Vorster, also known as the Church Planting Doctor.
Church Planting Doctor is a Registered Ministry in Australia. Any profits from the sale
of this course will be used to promote church planting around the world.
Scripture taken from the HOLY BIBLE, NEW INTERNATIONAL VERSION®. Copyright © 1973, 1978, 1984 Biblica. Used by permission of Zondervan.

❦ Created with Vellum

INTRODUCTION

When we look at the teachings of Jesus, we see that Jesus started by teaching His disciples about the values of the Kingdom. We all live in a certain culture. A culture is determined by the shared embracing of values.

> *"A culture is determined by the shared embracing of predetermined values."*
> Hendrik J. Vorster

JESUS TAUGHT HIS DISCIPLES VALUES

We all agree that the impact Jesus had on His Disciples through the way He discipled them was quite incredible. We would be wise to consider the key essential elements of His teaching of His Disciples. The first two things **Jesus taught**, and continued to teach His Disciples, was **the Values of the Kingdom of God** as well as accompanying **Spiritual Disciplines,** which would keep those values well rooted and maintained in the Believers' life.

When we look at the Gospel of Matthew, we see how Jesus called His Disciples together to teach them:

> *Matthew 5:1-2 (NIV) "[5:1] Now when he saw the crowds, he went up on a mountainside and sat down.* **His disciples came to him, [2] and he began to teach them,** *saying:"*

Jesus sat down with His Disciples and taught them about the values of the Kingdom of God, primarily through the Sermon on the Mount, but then throughout His time of discipling them over a three and a half year period.

The first phase of Discipleship deals with us becoming "Born again," and the second Phase of Discipleship deals with us putting down roots in our faith through developing spiritual disciplines as well as the establishment and grounding ourselves in the Values of the Kingdom of God.

Each kingdom has its own Culture built on commonly shared values.

Jesus came to establish the Kingdom of God. Each kingdom has its own culture that is built on commonly shared values. When we become children of God, we transition from the Kingdom of this world to the Kingdom of our Lord and Saviour, Jesus Christ. The Kingdom of God has its own values. The first thing we need to learn as Followers of Jesus Christ is what the Values of the Kingdom of God are, and how to affirm them in our lives.

A few years ago we migrated from South Africa to Australia. It was quite a process, one that I don't recommend to the faint-hearted, unless following the Call of God to do so. Once our qualifications, health checks and police clearances were accessed and accepted, we were granted residency visas in Australia, however, when we wanted to become Citizens, *we were required to learn, adopt and accept the cultural values of the Australian people*, before we could become Citizens.

The Kingdom of God operates on a similar principle of us having to accept the values before the blessings of the Kingdom could be enjoyed.

Jesus started the process of making His Disciples by teaching them the Values of the Kingdom of God, as well as Spiritual Disciplines that would keep those Values well rooted and maintained.

Cultures develop through the corporate upholding of values.

Todd Wilson, in his Book *"Dream Big"* explores the changing of a culture and states that there are primarily three ingredients to successful culture change: Values, Narratives and Behaviour.[1] He defines these as:

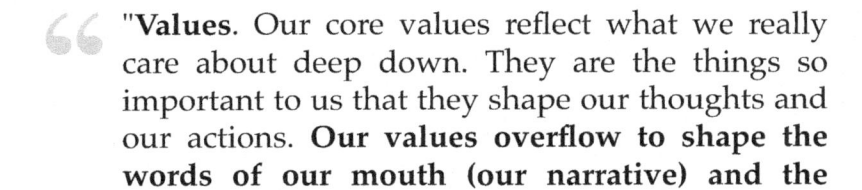

> "**Values**. Our core values reflect what we really care about deep down. They are the things so important to us that they shape our thoughts and our actions. **Our values overflow to shape the words of our mouth (our narrative) and the actions of our hands (our behaviours)."**

> "**Our narratives** are shaped by the language we use, the stories we tell, and how frequently we talk about and celebrate the things most important to us. Our narratives inspire others to embrace our values and engage on common mission with us."

> "**Our behaviours** are the things we actually do, including how and where we invest the time, talent, and financial resources entrusted to our care."[2]

Dr. Ralph Neighbour, or "uncle Ralph" as I affectionately know him, emphasized this area as one of the most important areas to develop in the making of a Disciple. He states, in his Book "Life Basic Training," that *"your beliefs mould your values, which directly influences your actions."*³

> *"Your beliefs mould your values, which directly influences your actions." Dr. Ralph W. Neighbour Jr.*

John the Baptist demanded the demonstration of a change of Values prior to Baptism.

For John the Baptist it was more important to baptise people who had a heart change, than baptising those who simply wanted to appear, on the outside and in front of the crowds, to have changed.

On one occasion he firmly addressed the crowds coming to be baptised, questioning the reason for their desire to be baptised. I love the way the Amplified Bible expounds on this powerful message. His message was clear: ***"Following your conversion, bear fruit consistent with the trees you've become."***

> Luke 3:8 (AMP) "[8] **Bear fruits that are deserving and consistent with [your] repentance** [*that is,* **conduct worthy of a heart changed**, *a heart abhorring sin*]. *And do not begin to say to yourselves, We have Abraham as our father; for I tell you that God is able from these stones to raise up descendants for Abraham."*

Jesus demanded a changed heart to express itself through a changed life.

For Jesus it was the assimilation of the Kingdom of God Values, which showed the world that true conversion took place. He both affirmed John's message and continually got to the core of Discipleship training by speaking of **good and bad trees** and the *required consistency between the tree and its fruit.*

> *Matthew 7:17-18, 20 (NKJV) "17 Even so,* **every good tree bears good fruit***, but a bad tree bears bad fruit. 18 A good tree cannot bear bad fruit, nor can a bad tree bear good fruit. 20 Therefore* **by their fruits you will know them.***"*

> *"The spiritual roots we develop will result in fruit that will be consistent with the trees we are." Hendrik J. Vorster*

The assimilation of Kingdom values, consistent with the conversion that took place inside of us, will have an outward effect on the "fruit" we bear. As we allow the Love of God to shine into our hearts, His Love will be seen by others (the world,) and it will show that we are His Disciples.

> *John 13:35 (NIV) "35 By this everyone will know that you are my disciples, if you love one another."*

Jesus called us to teach our Disciples what He taught His.

Finding Disciples is one thing, but *"teaching them to observe"* is another. Jesus called us to teach our Disciples the very things He taught His Disciples.

xiv | INTRODUCTION

ONLY DISCIPLE BORN AGAIN BELIEVERS!

Once you have a "Born Again" Believer then you can start the investment process of instilling the Values of the Kingdom of God in their life. Only those who have bowed their knees to the Lordship of Christ, and built their lives on Christ as their Rock and Foundation, will find true value in assimilating the Values of the Kingdom of God.

HAVE YOU EVER WONDERED WHERE TO START?

I always wondered where to start once people committed their lives to Christ, however when I looked at how Jesus did it, remembering that He started His Discipleship journey with people who left everything to follow Him, **I found that Jesus started by teaching His Disciples the Values of the Kingdom of God, and simultaneously spiritual Disciplines.**

Developing Spiritual Disciplines is like putting down spiritual roots. The result will be that as you learn and apply the Values of the Kingdom of God, you will bear fruit that will let everyone know the Vine you are grafted into.

Values are built into our lives by being intentional.

Values are those virtues, which have been added into our lives by intention. Embracing and living godly values build our character. Our character defines us.

> *James 1:25 (NIV) "²⁵ But **whoever looks intently into the perfect law** that gives freedom, and continues in it—not forgetting what they have heard, but doing it—they will be blessed in what they do."*

God desires for us to be intentional, both on contemplation as well as application.

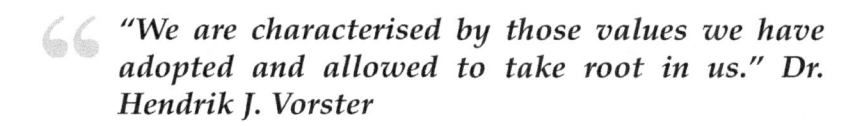

> "We are characterised by those values we have adopted and allowed to take root in us." Dr. Hendrik J. Vorster

Values are embraced in our minds first, before they become part of our hearts.

One famous writer suggests in one of her books that our bodies follow where our minds go. What we think about and give our attention to is what we will become. Proverbs says: **"As a man think in his heart, so is he."**

> *Philippians 4:8 "Finally, brethren, whatsoever things are true, whatsoever things are honest, whatsoever things are just, whatsoever things are pure, whatsoever things are lovely, whatsoever things are of good report; if there be any virtue, and if there be any praise, think on these things."*

> *Psalm 119:56 (NIV)* "[56] **This has been my practice:** *I obey your precepts."*

Values become part of our lives by practice.

The Apostle Paul taught his spiritual son, Timothy, to have a disciplined life and to pursue godliness.

> **1 Timothy 4:7** *(NIV) "Have nothing to do with godless myths and old wives' tales; rather,* **train yourself to be godly."**

> *"Values are the fruit we bear from the decisions we make, through our pursuits of following the example of Christ."* Hendrik J. Vorster

PART I

SPIRITUAL ROOTS

Spiritual Roots develop and grow when we establish Spiritual Disciplines and Kingdom Values in our lives. Establishing Values and Spiritual Disciplines concurrently, develops roots from which our faith will grow and mature. The more we embrace the Word of God, His Will, and His Holy Spirit's directive over our lives, the more we allow the Seed of the Word to grow deep and strong roots. Having strong roots are essential to growing a healthy and stable spiritual life.

Let us now take a journey into an understanding of the Spiritual Disciplines and the Values of the Kingdom of God.

In this Book we will explore **Values of the Kingdom of God**. To retain and maintain these Values in our lives we are required to develop Spiritual Disciplines concurrently.

SPIRITUAL DISCIPLINES

Spiritual Disciplines will ensure that we retain and maintain the Values we assimilate in our lives. Spiritual disciplines are habits, practices, and experiences that are designed to develop, grow, and strengthen our inner man. Spiritual disciplines build the capacity of our character and keep the values we aspire to assimilate into our lives, intact. Spiritual disciplines form the structure within which we train our soul to obey. Developing Spiritual Disciplines is like putting down roots into the places where you desire to draw your sustenance from. The Disciplines we develop will become pathways through which God will bring daily and consistent nourishment for our up building and strengthening.

> *"Spiritual disciplines are habits, practices, and experiences that are designed to develop, grow, and strengthen our inner man."* Dr. Hendrik J. Vorster

Values are born and developed in our lives by being rooted in a disciplined lifestyle of spiritual disciplines.

Jesus emphasised the value of the development of spiritual roots through the Parable of the Sower. What Jesus taught His Disciples was that, as soon as what the seed of the Word was sown and germinated, new Believers need to put down roots to sustain them through the trouble and persecution that would come on them as a consequence of their decision to follow Christ.

> *Psalms 1:1 (NIV)* "[3] **They are like trees along a riverbank** *bearing luscious fruit each season without fail. Their leaves shall never wither, and all they do shall prosper.*
>
> *Jeremiah 17:7-8 (NIV)* "[7] *But blessed is the man who trusts in the Lord and has made the Lord his hope and confidence.* [8] *He is like a tree planted along a riverbank, with its roots reaching deep into the water—a tree not bothered by the heat nor worried by long months of drought. Its leaves*

stay green, and it goes right on producing all its luscious fruit."

Put down roots in the right place

Everything that grows has roots. The bigger the tree, the deeper and stronger the roots grow. We all grow and put down roots to sustain the life we want to live. Putting down roots through life habits and practices, in the right places, is essential to living a fulfilled and fruitful life.

Putting down roots take time

We make time for the things we value. When we value spending time with God and love reading and meditating on His Word, we put our hope and confidence in Him to guide and direct us. By spending time with God, because we highly value His guidance and direction, we literally place our hope in Him. There are huge rewards for putting your hope and confidence in Him; it is that putting down of spiritual roots deep into the spiritual resources of God.

> *Matthew 13:5-6 (NIV) "Some fell on rocky places, where it did not have much soil. It sprang up quickly, because the soil was shallow. But when the sun came up, the plants were scorched, and* **they withered because they had no root."**

> *Matthew 13:20-21 (NIV) "The seed falling on rocky ground refers to someone who hears the word and at once receives it with joy.* **But since they have no root, they last only a short time.** *When trouble or persecution comes because of the word, they quickly fall away."*

Spiritual Disciplines are really the roots from which we will grow. When we are rooted in the right place, we will grow. Having, and developing, spiritual roots in the right practices and disciplines will most certainly ensure a lifetime of healthy growth and unending fruit bearing. It is essential to disciple new Believers into understanding the importance of putting down roots for them to grow spiritually.

Develop godly roots

Spiritual Disciplines are really the roots from which we will grow. When we are rooted in the right place, we will grow. Having, and developing, spiritual roots in the right practices and disciplines will most certainly ensure a lifetime of healthy growth and an unending fruit bearing life. It is essential to disciple new Believers into an understanding of – and the development of - the spiritual disciplines.

If you invest time in evil things, don't be surprised when evil habits, characteristics and behaviour pops up in your life. By spending time and watching bad moral movies, television programs; or spending time with the wrong friends; or reading the wrong books, blogs or websites, is investing into roots that will not bring forth good fruit or the good, godly nature you desire.

If you invest time intentionally into developing a good and godly character, built on good moral values, and being a good role model for others to follow, then you will invest time into eternally lasting practices.

Roots are determined by what you practice and give time to

We all aspire to be people of high integrity, with well-balanced personalities, good character, and pleasant to be around with natures. You develop the character, nature and behaviour you aspire for by investing time and disciplined practice into developing that character.

Jesus taught His Disciples the importance of having and developing roots, through the Parable of the Sower. Just as in the Parable of the Sower, the second phase of growth and development in the Believers' faith, is the development of spiritual roots. The writer to the Romans, also speak about the roots.

> *Romans 11:16 (NIV) "if the part of the dough offered as firstfruits is holy, then the whole batch is holy;* **if the root is holy, so are the branches.***"*

WHAT WE LEARN HERE IS both the importance of having "**holy roots,**" but also the impact holy roots have on the branches and ultimately on the fruit it will bear. The Apostle Paul addresses this same matter with the church in Colossae. He exhorts them to *"continue to live their lives in Him"*. How? ***"By being rooted and built up in Him."***

> *Colossians 2:6-7 (NIV) "So then, just as you received Christ Jesus as Lord, continue to live your lives in Him,* **rooted and built up in Him***, strengthened in the faith as you were taught, and overflowing with thankfulness."*

This same message is brought to the church in Ephesus; the message of *"being rooted"*.

> *Ephesians 3:17 (NIV) "so that Christ may dwell in your hearts through faith. And I pray that you,* **being rooted and established in love,***"*

When we develop spiritual disciplines, we develop spiritual roots.

The Apostle Paul taught his disciple, Timothy, to train himself to be godly. Developing spiritual disciplines is to train oneself to be godly. What we learn from the Bible is that it is essential equip yourself, train yourself, and develop yourself in Him. The duty is ours to develop a disciplined walk with God.

> *1 Timothy 4:7 (NIV) "7 Have nothing to do with godless myths and old wives' tales; rather,* **train yourself to be godly.***"*

DEFINING SPIRITUAL DISCIPLINES

Richard Foster published a masterpiece in 1978 called *"Celebration of Discipline."* He defined spiritual disciplines and explored them under three parts, namely inward disciplines, outward disciplines and corporate disciplines. **The inward disciplines** he defined are: *prayer, fasting, meditation and study.* **The outward disciplines** are: *simplicity, solitude, submission and service.* **The corporate disciplines** are: *confession, worship, guidance and celebration.* His book really helped me think about having a disciplined walk as well as expand my disciplines.

Corine Gatti published a blog on Beliefnet.com, outlining and suggesting 7 spiritual disciplines for us to pursue on a daily basis. They are: Read the Word, Meditate on God, Worship, Seek Forgiveness, Reflection, Submission, and Use what you've learnt. Though simplified, it still helps those who start their journey into disciplines.

A third person I wish to mention is **Donald Whitney**. He published *"Spiritual Disciplines for the Christian life."* The disciplines he proposes are: Bible intake, Prayer, Worship, Evangelism, Serving, Stewardship, Fasting, Silence and Solitude, Journaling, Learning, and Perseverance in the Disciplines.

One thing seems abundantly clear from these three is that

they all agree on the importance of a daily interaction with the Word of God, Prayer, Worship, Sharing of your faith, Fasting, Simplified living, Stewardship, and Service.

New Testament Practitioners

It seems from the impact that the early Church had that they had a few practices, which positioned them for such a revival atmosphere where people were added to the Church on a daily basis.

We also have a number of examples from that of the spiritual Disciplines of the Apostles. As the Church grew the complexities of ministry grew, however, what set the Apostles apart was their discipline to keep their Spiritual Disciplines undisturbed. Almost on every occasion the Apostles are mentioned it is connected with them going for prayer, busy praying or as a result of them praying and ministering the Word of God that awesome things happened.

> *Acts 6:4 (NIV) "4 **and we will give our attention to prayer and the ministry of the word.**"*

Acts 2 verses 42-46 highlight some of the spiritual practices of the Believers in the Book of Acts.

> *Acts 2:42-47 (NIV) "42 **They devoted themselves to the apostles' teaching** and **to fellowship**, to the **breaking of bread** and **to prayer**. 43 Everyone was filled with awe at the many wonders and signs performed by the apostles. 44 **All the believers were together** and **had everything in common**. 45 **They sold property and possessions to give to anyone who had need**. 46 Every day **they continued to meet together** in the temple courts. **They broke bread in their homes** and ate together*

*with glad and sincere hearts, 47 **praising God and enjoying the favor of all the people**. And the Lord added to their number daily those who were being saved."*

In this portion of Scripture we observe at least seven spiritual disciplines, which existed in the early Church. They practiced these disciplines daily. They gave themselves to it wholly. **The Spiritual Disciplines** of devoting yourself to **the Word of God** (*Apostle's Teachings*), **worship** (*fellowship*), **Communion** (*Breaking of Bread*), **Prayer, Simplicity** (*had everything in common*), **Stewardship** (*They sold property and possessions to give to anyone who had need*) and **Witnessing** (*enjoying the favor of all the people.*) The amazing thing about this testimony and example is that the Lord crowned their private and corporate devotion, by *"daily adding to their numbers those who were being saved."*

IN MY BOOK on Spiritual Disciplines we explore and learn how to develop each Spiritual Discipline, and how to assimilate them into our lives. My Book on Spiritual Disciplines is called: **"Spiritual Disciplines of the Kingdom of God."**

I pray that you too will be **"rooted in Christ,"** and that you will grow into a mighty **"Oak of righteousness."**

2

VALUES DEFINED

> "Values are the fruit we bear, of the Faith we profess and practice."

*E*very Family has family values. Our lives are built upon these values. Values are the fruit we bear, affirming our allegiance and reliance on God. It is that constant demonstration of our faith and the foundation we build our lives on.

I pray that you will be intentional in building these Values into your life, as it will become one of the biggest testimonies you will carry, in your life, of the Power of God to change lives.

Very few things have such incredible convincing power than a changed life. Let us not just tell people of Christ; let us live the change He brought into our lives. This is only possible as we connect our Faith in God to the renewal work of the Holy Spirit, through being "Born Again," and learning and applying these Kingdom Values. Enjoy this exhilarating journey!

There are many Values in the Kingdom of God, however,

for the purpose of this Book, I narrowed them down to 52 Kingdom Values.

Defining the Values

VALUES, morals, virtues, ethics, principles, manners, protocol and etiquette, all add ultimately, in various proportions, to the forming of our Character.

Character

The Character of our Nature is formed by the intentional and proportionate appropriation of values and manners; our upholding of virtues; remaining true to our principles; and our expressed understanding and conduct in applying protocol and etiquette, forge our character until we are proved to be Sound, Solid and Time-Tested.

Values

Values are those culturally and socially acceptable good standards, high morals, noble ethics, sound principles, sacred beliefs, and biblical tenets you hold in high worth and importance, and which, if upheld, will help you live a fruitful and fulfilled life.

THE BUSINESS DICTIONARY defines Values as:

> *"Values are important and lasting **beliefs** or ideals shared by the members of a culture about what is good or bad and desirable or undesirable. These **Values** have a major influence on a person's behavior and attitude and serve as broad guidelines in all situations."* [1]

Morals

Morals relate to the culturally acceptable principles or rules of right conduct or the acceptable societal distinction between right and wrong. Morals relate to the ethical, **moral** attitudes applied to life. Good social morals keeps one socially held in high regard.

Ethics

Ethics is the disciplined application of moral duties and obligations. The application of ethics shows the morals and principles by which one lives. Ethics gives expression to the moral character one determined in one's life. Being ethical is conducting oneself consistently with high morals.

The Merriam-Webster Dictionary defines ethics as: *"Ethics is the discipline dealing with what is good and bad and with moral duty and obligation. Ethics is a set of moral principles: a theory or system of moral values."*

Wikipedia defines ethics as: *"Ethics or moral philosophy is a branch of philosophy that involves systematizing, defending, and recommending concepts of right and wrong conduct. ... Ethics seeks to resolve questions of human morality by defining concepts such as good and evil, right and wrong, virtue and vice, justice and crime."*[2]

The English word "*ethics*" is derived from an Ancient Greek word, *êthikos*, which means "***relating to one's character***". The Ancient Greek adjective *êthikos* is itself derived from another Greek word, the noun *êthos* meaning "***character, disposition***".[3]

Rushworth Kidder states that *"standard definitions*

of ethics have typically included such phrases as 'the science of the ideal human character' or 'the science of moral duty'".[4]

Richard William Paul and Linda Elder define ethics as *"a set of concepts and principles that guide us in determining what behavior helps or harms sentient creatures".*[5]

The Cambridge Dictionary of Philosophy states that the word "ethics" is *"commonly used interchangeably with 'morality' ... and sometimes it is used more narrowly to mean the moral principles of a particular tradition, group or individual."*[6]

Paul and Elder state that most people confuse ethics with behaving in accordance with social conventions, religious beliefs and the law and don't treat ethics as a stand-alone concept.[7]

Our conduct ultimately reveal the Values we stand for

When people observe your conduct, they determine the principles, the morals, the ethics and beliefs by which you live.

Virtues

Virtues are those asserted good and admirable qualities of integrity that are of high moral standard. Virtue speaks of chastity and pureness in motive, actions and thought. Virtues' living are ascribed to those who uphold the moral high ground. Virtue shows behaviour of high moral standard.

> The Catechism of the Catholic Church defines virtue as *"a habitual and firm disposition to do good."*[1] *Traditionally, The seven Christian virtues or heavenly virtues combine the four classical cardinal virtues of prudence, justice,*

temperance and courage (or fortitude) with the three theological virtues of faith, hope and charity,"[8]

"Virtue is moral excellence. A virtue is a trait or quality that is deemed to be morally good and thus is valued as a foundation of principle and good moral being."[9]

To be virtues is to habitually dispose oneself in humility, kindness, moderation, chastity, patience, bigheartedness and diligence.

Principles

Principles are those beliefs we so deeply embrace, that it influences the way we behave.

Collins Dictionary defines Principle as: *"A principle is a general belief that you have about the way you should behave, which influences your behaviour."*[10]

Wikipedia defines Principle as: *"A principle is a concept or value that is a guide for behavior or evaluation."*[11]

Manners

Manners, otherwise referred to as Etiquette, are in many aspects an unwritten, culturally acceptable code of behavior that distinguishes between acceptable and appropriate behavior within specific social, societal and group settings. Our Manners determine whether our behavior is appropriate and acceptable, or not.

Wikipedia defines etiquette as: *"Etiquette, is a code of behavior that delineates expectations for social behavior according to* *contemporary conventional norms within a society, social class, or group."*[12]

Protocol

Protocol refers to the system of suitable manners, etiquette and conduct to be shown in a variety of formal situations. Protocol both encapsulates the conduct, and procedures, to be followed within the determined formal settings.

Definition of protocol for English Language Learners. *: "a system of rules that explain the correct conduct and procedures to be followed in formal situations."*[13]

We do what we value

For our purpose, in exploring Values, it is essential that we have a broader embracing understanding, hence the defining of some other related and interwoven aspects, which together form our character.

Values form the root system of our character.

All of these, in various degrees, support or stem from the values we hold. Values form the root system of our character. *We do what we value*. We are what we value. There is great consistency between what we value and who we are, and that forms the basis of what people see and belief to be true in us.

MATURITY COMES THROUGH OBEDIENCE

*I*n conclusion on preparing ourselves for this journey into the Values of the Kingdom of God, let us consider the most essential discipline in the Discipleship Journey, the discipline of Obedience.

Jesus commissioned us to obey

Firstly, Jesus taught His Disciples the *Spiritual Discipline of Obedience*. Part of the process of Discipleship is to teach our disciples *"to obey everything"* Jesus taught us.

> *Matthew 28:20 (NKJV)* "20 **teaching them to observe all things that I have commanded you**; *and lo, I am with you always, even to the end of the age." Amen."*

> *Matthew 28:20 (NIV)* "*²⁰* **and teaching them to obey everything I have commanded you.** *And surely I am with you always, to the very end of the age."*

> *Matthew 28:20 (LB) "*²⁰*and **then teach these new disciples to obey all the commands I have given you;** and be sure of this—that I am with you always, even to the end of the world."*
>
> *Matthew 28:20 (The Passion Translation) "* ²⁰ *And **teach them to faithfully follow**[i]** all that I have commanded you.** And never forget that I am with you every day, even to the completion of this age."*

No Discipleship is possible without the intention and commitment to follow through, by taking those who accepted Christ as Lord, to a place of fully obeying the commands of the Lord Jesus.

We all are committed to obey the rules of the Road

A simple comparable example, but truly applicable, is to draw a comparison with the demand we place on people to apply and obey all the rules of the road in driving. **As much as what full obedience to the road rules are demanded and expected** by every person who intend using the road as a way of going from one place safely to another, **in the same way full obedience to the teachings of Jesus is demanded** and expected in the Kingdom of God.

Jesus modeled obedience

Jesus practiced and modeled obedience unto death. Our disciplines are not just for a season or for a specific event, but it is an inward aptitude of discipline for this life.

> *Philippians 2:8 (NKJV) "8 And being found in appearance as a man, **He** humbled Himself and*

> *became obedient to the point of death, even the death of the cross."*

Jesus was obedient unto death. It is ours to follow in His footsteps.

> *John 14:23-24 (NIV) "23 Jesus replied, "**Anyone who loves me will obey my teaching.** My Father will love them, and we will come to them and make our home with them. 24 Anyone who does not love me will not obey my teaching. These words you hear are not my own; they belong to the Father who sent me."*

Jesus learnt obedience through His suffering.

Disciplining ourselves daily towards submission and obedience to the Word, Will and Purpose of God will most certainly unlock great favor and blessing over our lives. This is the Promise God gave us in Deuteronomy 28 verses 1-13, for full submission and obedience.

> *Deuteronomy 28:1-2 (NKJV) ""Now it shall come to pass, **if you diligently obey the voice of the Lord your God, to observe carefully all His commandments** which I command you today, that the Lord your God will set you high above all nations of the earth. ² And **all these blessings shall come upon you and overtake you, because you obey the voice of the Lord your God:**"*

Joshua and Caleb obeyed and conquered the Promised Land

Joshua and Caleb had the faith to obey, and therefor entered into the Promised land God promised them.

> *Hebrews 4:2 (NIV) "² For we also have had the good news proclaimed to us, just as they did; but the message they heard was of no value to them, because they did not share* **the faith of those who obeyed**.*"*

When we combine our Faith in God with Obedience, we too will enter our Promised lands.

Faith to Obey

It takes faith to obey, and faith is expressed by the way we obey.

Spiritual Maturity

Putting things into practice and obeying God will bring us to spiritual Maturity. No spiritual maturity is ever possible without practicing and living the values, and practicing the disciplines taught in this Discipleship Journey through the Teachings of Jesus and the Bible.

> *Hebrews 5: 12-14 (NIV) "¹² In fact, though by this time you ought to be teachers, you need someone to teach you the elementary truths of God's word all over again. You need milk, not solid food! ¹³ Anyone who lives on milk, being still an infant, is not acquainted with the teaching about righteousness. ¹⁴ But* **solid food is for the mature, who by constant use have trained themselves to distinguish** *good from evil."*
>
> *Hebrews 5:12-14 (AMPC) "¹² For even though by*

*this time you ought to be teaching others, you actually need someone to teach you over again the very first principles of God's Word. You have come to need milk, not solid food. ¹³ For everyone who continues to feed on milk is obviously inexperienced and unskilled in the doctrine of righteousness (**of conformity to the divine will in purpose, thought, and action**), for he is a mere infant [not able to talk yet]! ¹⁴ But **solid food is for full-grown men, for those whose senses and mental faculties are trained by practice to discriminate and distinguish between what is morally good and noble and what is evil and contrary either to divine or human law.**"*

When we look at this portion in God's Word, we see a number of essential truths that will bring us to Spiritual Maturity.

1. We need someone to teach us.

*Hebrews 5:12 (AMPC) "¹² For even though **by this time you ought to be teaching others**, you actually need someone to teach you over again the very first principles of God's Word. You have come to need milk, not solid food."*

The first is that *we all need,* as you did by going through this course, *someone to teach you the elementary truths* of God's Word. In this portion the writer to the Hebrews actually speaks in the negative tone as he addresses Believers who were supposed to be Mature, and Teachers of the truth, however, because *"they have become dull"* in their *"[spiri-*

tual] hearing and sluggish [even slothful in achieving spiritual insight", they needed to be taught again. May we learn and keep the things we have learned in practice in our lives.

2. Spiritual Maturity comes through conforming to the Will of God.

> *Hebrews 5:13 (AMPC) "*^{13}* For everyone who continues to feed on milk is obviously inexperienced and unskilled in the doctrine of righteousness (**of conformity to the divine will in purpose, thought, and action**), for he is a mere infant [not able to talk yet]!"*

Secondly, we learn that to be mature requires us to be experienced and skilled in *"the doctrine of righteousness"* which means that we have *"**conformed to the divine will of God in purpose, thought and action**"*. I want to encourage you to make a heartfelt decision to conform to the Will of God.

Conforming means to imitate, follow and obey.

May we obey, follow and imitate the example set to us by our Lord and Saviour Jesus Christ. I love the expansion of the Amplified Bible when it says: *"**conformed to the divine will of God in purpose, thought and action**"*. Maturity comes to those who build the Spiritual values and disciplines into their lives purposefully, both in thought and in their actions.

3. Spiritual maturity comes by practice and training to discriminate and to distinguish.

> *Hebrews 5:14 (AMPC) "*^{14}* But solid food is for full-*

*grown men, **for those whose senses and mental faculties are trained by practice** to discriminate and distinguish between what is morally good and noble and what is evil and contrary either to divine or human law."*

In the third place we see that Spiritual **maturity comes by practicing and training** our *"senses and mental faculties"*, *"to discriminate and to distinguish"* between what is *"morally good and noble"*.

For us, this is our desire to please the Lord in everything. What the Bible teaches us here is that **we need to apply our senses and mental faculties to pursue Spiritual Maturity**. Allow the Holy Spirit to speak to you and to have His way in developing and working in you. By taking these teachings of the Lord Jesus, and the Bible, and applying them as a standard by which we distinguish and assess our intentions, actions and practices, we will become mature and full-grown men in Christ.

One of the things that made the Disciples distinct from the rest of the people was that people could see in their actions that they have been with Jesus.

*Acts 4:13 (NIV) "¹³ When they saw the courage of Peter and John and realized that they were unschooled, ordinary men, **they were astonished and they took note that these men had been with Jesus."***

WHEN PEOPLE LOOK at our courage, our values, our disciplines, they must recognize that we are obedient Followers and Believers in Jesus.

PART II

HUMILITY

Definition

Humility is the quality of having a modest or subjected view of one's importance.

Scriptural teaching

Matthew 5:3 (NIV 1984) 3 "**Blessed are the poor in spirit**, *for theirs is the kingdom of heaven.*

Matthew 5:3 (AMP) ³ "Blessed [spiritually prosperous, happy, to be admired] are **the poor in spirit** [those devoid of spiritual arrogance, **those who regard themselves as insignificant**], for theirs is the kingdom of heaven [both now and forever]."

> *1 Peter 5:5-6 (NIV 1984) 5 "Young men, in the same way* **be submissive to those who are older. All of you, clothe yourselves with humility toward one another**, *because, "God opposes the proud but gives grace to the humble." 6* **Humble yourselves,** *therefore, under God's mighty hand, that he may lift you up in due time."*

> *Philippians 2:3 (NIV 1984) 3 Do nothing out of selfish ambition or vain conceit, but* **in humility consider others better than yourselves.**

> *Philippians 2:8 (NIV 1984) 8 And being found in appearance as a man,* **He humbled himself** *and became obedient to death—even death on a cross!*

Characteristic explained:

HUMILITY IS the first Value or Characteristic Jesus taught His Disciples. A Kingdom operates significantly different than a democratically run country. In a Kingdom there is only One Ruler and doing His or Her will is all that matters. In the Kingdom of God there is One King and His Name is Jesus. In this Kingdom, of which we are part of since being Born Again, doing His Will is the only thing that counts and is prized.

Words that describe humility are: unpretentiousness, modesty, meekness and even shyness. It requires tremendous humility to be apart of a Kingdom. It requires us to wholeheartedly submit and obey everything He said, and through the Holy Spirit's guidance directs us to do. Through submission and whole-hearted obedience we give expression to our heartfelt humility. This value characterizes every follower of

Jesus. We become known for our total submission to His will as taught to us through the Bible.

Life application:

The best expression we could give to this value in our lives is to demonstrate it through our subjective and deferent living to the Lordship of Jesus, the Word and the Will of God, in every area of our lives. Deferent living implies expressing the Will of God, as defined in the teachings of Jesus, in our every action, reaction, in words or by our deeds. Our whole lives should be a display of our submission to the Lordship of Christ. Humility is expressed through our display and referencing the Values of the Kingdom of God. Obey the laws of the Bible and that of the country we live in.

Prayer:

"Lord Jesus, I humble myself and submit myself to Your Supreme Rulership in my life. I bow my knees and my Will to Your Lordship and commit myself to Your Will and putting all Your Commands into practice in my life. I humbly pray this in Jesus Name!"

MOURNFULNESS

Definition:

Mournfulness is the value of penitent and reflective living. Penitence is the applied value of humbly and honestly assessing one's actions before God, always with a willingness to acknowledge our wrongs and to follow through with repentance and seeking true forgiveness. This penitent action reflects the value of mournfulness.

Scriptures:

Matthew 5:4 (NIV 1984) 4 **Blessed are those who mourn**, *for they will be comforted.*

Luke 18:13 (NIV) [13] "But the tax collector stood at a distance. He would not even look up to heaven, but beat his breast and said, **'God, have mercy on me, a sinner.***'*

Psalms 51:1-4 (NIV) [51:1] **Have mercy on me, O** *God, according to your unfailing love;* **according to Your great compassion blot out my transgressions.** *[2] Wash away all my iniquity and cleanse me from my sin. [3] For* **I know my transgressions, and my sin is always before me.**[4] **Against you,** *you only,* **have I sinned and done what is evil in your sight**, *so that you are proved right when you speak and justified when you judge.*

Characteristic explained:

Mournfulness is sometimes described by words like: penitence, repentance, remorsefulness, self-reproach, self-accusation, shame, or sorrowfulness.

> The Matthew Henry Dictionary comments and defines this "mourning" as: *"That godly sorrow which works true repentance, watchfulness, a humble mind, and continual dependence for acceptance on the mercy of God in Christ Jesus, with constant seeking the Holy Spirit, to cleanse away the remaining evil, seems here to be intended."*

Life Application:

This value is firmly established in our lives when we always keep ourselves open to correction without arguing for the mere fact that we might actually be in the wrong. Rather be wronged than being known as a self-righteous, never wrong, always right, can't be corrected, kind of a person. This value defines us as children of the Kingdom of God. May this heart attitude of penitence before God be carried out into every conversation and encounter we have with others.

. . .

It is a beautiful thing to observe in Believers when they carry in themselves a spirit of penitence. Always keep an open heart and mind to carefully assess your life in view of God's Word with a repentant heart.

Prayer:

"Lord Jesus, I open myself to allow Your Holy Spirit to search and purge my every thought and way, because I desire to live in right standing with You. I have no desire to harbor sin in my life, but choose to respond to the conviction of the Holy Spirit's voice inside of me with confession, repentance and a heartfelt altering of my ways to comply with Your Will and Word."

3

MEEKNESS

Definition:

Meekness is the consistent characteristic of submissiveness. Meekness is to present oneself in every situation as one who lives under the rule and directive of another. Meekness is living in absolute self-surrender to the Will of God.

Scriptures:

Matthew 5:5 (NIV 1984) 5 **Blessed are the meek**, *for they will inherit the earth.*

Matthew 6:10 (NIV) [10] **your kingdom come, your will be done** *on earth as it is in heaven.*

John 4:34 (NIV) [34] "My food," said Jesus, "is **to do the will of him** *who sent me and to finish his work."*

John 6:38 (NIV) [38] For I have come down from heaven not to do my will but **to do the will of him who sent me.** *"*

Isaiah 53:7 (NIV) [7] He was oppressed and afflicted, yet **he did not open his mouth;** *he was led* **like a lamb to the slaughter,** *and as a sheep before her shearers is silent, so he did not open his mouth.*

Characteristic explained:

Meekness is expressed in living with a spirit of submissiveness, for the sake of Christ. Resistance, in-submission, self-will, and sometimes rebellion express the opposite of meekness. Meekness is seen when we choose to rather be the least, or wronged, than fighting and resisting the wrong done to us. Christ was *"like a Lamb before the slaughter"* He did not open His mouth, or resisted the injustice done to Him. Meekness requires the absolute surrender of any form of entitlement. The strength of meekness is seen in its full reliance on the God who sees and will let justice be done in the end.

Life Application:

We are meek when we submit ourselves to the Will of God and to rather trust Him for a favorable outcome than to fight for what we believe to be right.

Joseph is one of the greatest examples to us of a man who lived in absolute meekness, and entrusted himself to God regardless of the injustices done to him. We show meekness when we give expression to everything we do that we will only do what the Lord would have us do and say. **Moses is possibly another great example** of someone who entrusted himself entirely to the Will and determination of the Lord, especially when God determined that he would not enter the

Promised Land himself. **Jesus is our Ultimate example of Meekness** for His total subjection to the Will of the Father in dying on the Cross of Calvary. Obliging Himself to the Will of God entirely is possibly one of the greatest examples to us of being meek and submitting to the Will of God.

Prayer:

We might pray: *"Lord, I fully submit myself to Your Supreme Rulership in and over my life. Whatever you determine best in my life is what I want."*

SPIRITUAL PASSION

Definition:

To have spiritual passion is to fully express oneself in what you belief and stand for. Spiritual Passion is expressed when we give ourselves fully to our faith and His way of living.

Scriptures:

*Matthew 5:6 (NIV 1984) 6 Blessed are those who **hunger and thirst for righteousness**, for they will be filled.*

*1 Timothy 4:12, 15 (NIV) [12] Don't let anyone look down on you because you are young, but **set an example for the believers** in speech, in life, in love, in faith and in purity. [15] **Be diligent in these matters; give yourself wholly to them**, so that everyone may see your progress."*

*Romans 12:11 (NIV) "[11] Never be lacking in zeal, but **keep your spiritual fervor**, serving the Lord.*

Characteristic explained:

Words, which are sometimes associated with defining spiritual passion, are: eagerness, zeal, enthusiasm, excitement, spiritedness, fervency, fascination and obsession. To have spiritual passion is to be wholly sold out to what you belief and stand for. It is to be totally in love with the One you gave your life to. There should be no doubt to anyone who knows your Name that you are a Believer in Jesus Christ and that you are passionately pursuing Him and desire everything He has to offer. Spiritual passion is seen in the way in which we pursue Him and His Word, and the concurrent way in which we pursue the application of these values into our lives.

Life Application:

Spiritual Passion characterizes those who through their words, actions and deeds show their hunger and thirst for more of God, and His Word. May our spiritual fervour and pursuit of Him, and growth in Him, be visible to everyone. Apollos, a Follower of Jesus, was such a man of whom we read in Acts 18 verse 25. The Apostle Paul exhibited such spiritual fervour as we read about his zeal in Colossians 1 verse 28. James 5 verse 16 speaks of the fervent prayers of a righteous man. It accomplishes a lot. May we be fervent in our faith and worship of God.

Prayer:

"Dear Lord, may my zeal and the fervor with which I serve You

never fade or wane away, but let me always pursue you, through action and deeds, with a never ceasing, never waning hunger and thirst for more of You in my Life!"

MERCIFULNESS

Definition:

Mercy is the ability to consistently practice forbearance and leniency towards those who are failing and falling.

Scriptures:

Matthew 5:7 (NIV 1984) 7 **Blessed are the merciful**, *for they will be shown mercy.*

Luke 6:36 (NIV) "36 **Be merciful**, *just as your Father is merciful."*

Deuteronomy 4:31 (NIV) "31 For **the Lord your God is a merciful God**; *he will not abandon or destroy you or forget the covenant with your ancestors, which he confirmed to them by oath."*

James 2:13 (NIV) "13 because judgment without mercy will be shown to anyone who has not been merciful. **Mercy triumphs over judgment.***"*

Characteristic explained:

To be merciful is to be full of forbearance towards others as they face their shortcomings and failures. Words that best describe mercy are: compassion, pity, forgiveness, kindness and sympathy. Mercy is being generous in sympathy and expressed by a showing of caring and understanding. Mercy is being loving towards those in misery. Mercy is to possess a forgiving spirit toward those who sin against you. This virtue develops **"out of our own personal experience of the mercy of God.**

Life Application:

We are merciful when we fill ourselves with an understanding and forbearance towards others, that they might fail and fall. Mercy is best understood when we carefully consider how we desire God to deal with us, and treat us, when we come before Him with, knowing that he knows our every thought, action and word. We desire God to be gracious, compassionate, understanding and forgiving when we've messed up. May we find the Grace of God welled up in us to such an extent that we might deal with others in that same gracious and compassionate way. May we deal with the failures and shortcomings of others in a sympathetic and caringly understanding way. This is being merciful. Mercy is shown when we are being a Good Samaritan like we read in Luke 10:25-37. Jesus forgave those who crucified Him as we read in Luke 23:34. Stephen forgave those who stoned him as we read in Acts 7:60. In the "Our Father" Jesus spoke about forgiving those who sinned against us. Being Merciful.

Prayer:

"Lord Jesus, may I embrace myself with the same kind of forbearance that I expect You to have towards me every day. May I be full of mercy and ready to be gracious and compassionate to those who fall and fail around me today."

PURITY

Definition:

Purity is characterized by freedom from immorality, adultery and sinful contamination, and is a value of the Kingdom of God.

Scripture:

Matthew 5:8 (NIV 1984) 8 **Blessed are the pure in heart**, *for they will see God.*

Psalms 24:3-5 (NIV) [3] Who may ascend the hill of the LORD? Who may stand in his holy place? **[4] He who has clean hands and a pure heart**, *who does not lift up his soul to an idol or swear by what is false. [5] He will receive blessing from the LORD and vindication from God his Saviour.*

PURITY | 43

> *Philippians 4:8 (NIV) [8] Finally, brothers, whatever is true, whatever is noble, whatever is right,* **whatever is pure**, *whatever is lovely, whatever is admirable—if anything is excellent or praiseworthy—* **think about such things**.
>
> *1 Timothy 1:5 (NIV) [5]* **The goal of this command is love, which comes from a pure heart** *and a good conscience and a sincere faith. (2 Timothy 2:20.)*
>
> *1 Timothy 4:12 (NIV) [12] Don't let anyone look down on you because you are young, but* **set an example for the believers** *in speech, in life, in love, in faith and* **in purity**.
>
> *I Thessalonians 5:22* **"Abstain from all appearance of evil."**
>
> *Matthew 5:29-30 (NIV 1984) 29 If your right eye causes you to sin, gouge it out and throw it away.* **It is better for you to lose one part of your body than for your whole body to be thrown into hell.** *30 And if your right hand causes you to sin, cut it off and throw it away. It is better for you to lose one part of your body than for your whole body to go into hell.*
>
> *Psalms 51:10 (NIV)* **"Create in me a pure heart**, *O God, and renew a steadfast spirit within me.*

Characteristic explained:

Purity is associated with cleanness, wholesomeness, moral goodness, piety, uprightness, decency, worthiness, innocence, chastity and virtue. Purity is the result of living truthfully to

God and yourself. Purity is the state of thought in which we are uncorrupted by worldly pleasures or passions. Fearing God, and living according to His Word, keeps our hearts pure. Psalms 19:9, and 119:9 gives us good affirmative confirmation of the impact of keeping our lives pure. Our thoughts ultimately determine how we value purity. Our thoughts determine the seat *"chastity"* will have in our hearts.

Life Application:

Purity is seen in us by what we observe, speak about, and allow access into our lives through our senses. In other words, when people visit your house they will quickly see how pure and uncontainable you keep your life by seeing what television programs you watch, the books you have in your house, the movies you watch, the stories you tell and the things which drives your passion. We need to ensure that the channels, through which we feed our mind, and ultimately our hearts, need to be clean and uncontaminated. Whatever we feed our senses with is what we fill our thoughts with.

Psalms 15 verse 26 encourages us to have thoughts that are pleasing to the Lord. You see, so often people are judged by what they do, but in reality, the body follows where the mind went first, and once the mind digested evil and wrong paths, the body follows. I pray that we will be those who will pursue purity in our minds and protect our hearts from being corrupted with the things of the world.

Purity is also an outflow of the sanctifying work of the Holy Spirit. As we allow His cleansing and purifying work to continue in our lives, we become the men and woman God desired us to be – Pure.

Prayer:

"Lord, create in me a pure heart. May my thoughts and inten-

tions be pure and wholesome today. May I guard the thoughts of my heart and my mind. Holy Spirit. purify me and sanctify me through and through that all I can think about is whatever is pure, good, up-building and wholesome thoughts, affecting every way I respond and act."

PEACEMAKER

Definition:

A peacemaker is someone who actively steps up in every adversarial situation to work towards a peaceful outcome. Peacemakers are reconciliatory in action.

Scriptures:

Matthew 5:9 (NIV 1984) 9 **Blessed are the peacemakers**, *for they will be called sons of God.*

James 3:18 (NIV) [18] **Peacemakers who sow in peace** *raise a harvest of righteousness.*

Romans 14:19 (NIV) [19] **Let us** *therefore* **make every effort to do what leads to peace** *and to mutual edification.*

Romans 12:18 (NIV) [18] If it is possible, as far as it depends on you, **live at peace with everyone.**

Psalms 34:14 (NIV) [14] Turn from evil and do good; **seek peace and pursue it.**

Acts 7:26 (NIV) [26] The next day **Moses** *came upon two Israelites who were fighting.* **He tried to reconcile them** *by saying, 'Men, you are brothers; why do you want to hurt each other?'*

2 Corinthians 5:19-20 (NIV) [19] that God was reconciling the world to himself in Christ, not counting men's sins against them. And **he has committed to us the message of reconciliation.** *[20] We are therefore Christ's ambassadors, as though God were making his appeal through us.* **We implore you on Christ's behalf: Be reconciled to God.**

Ephesians 4:3 (NIV) [3] **Make every effort to keep the unity of the Spirit through the bond of peace.**

Characteristic explained:

Being a peacemaker is being someone who seeks to bring adversaries together and to earnestly seek to establish reconciliation between them. Words that are strongly associated with peacemaking are: negotiator, arbitrator, mediator, diplomat, appeaser, go-between, and pacifier.

Dustin S. in his blog on desiringgod.org gives a wonderful summary on a "peacemaker." He states: "A peacemaker is someone who experiences the peace of God (Philippians 4:7) because he is at peace (Romans 5:1) with the God of peace (Philippians 4:9) through the Prince of peace (Isaiah 9:6), who, indeed, is our peace (Ephesians 2:14), and who therefore seeks to live at peace with all others (Romans 12:18) and proclaims the gospel of peace (Ephesians 6:15) so that others might have joy and peace in believing (Romans 15:13)."

Believers are those who constantly seek to bring peace in troubled situations. They are also those who seek to help people to find peace with God.

Life Application:

It is hard to help others to be reconciled if you are still struggling in your own life. A Peacemaker first needs to have peace in his/her own heart, having been reconciled with God, before he/she could help others to be reconciled with God and fellow man. A peacemaker constantly steps into the gap to help remedy adversarial situations. We would soon become known as Peacemakers when we engage ourselves on a consistent basis to work towards peace. Seeking peace does not mean that we seek what we think is right, but what is best to defuse the situation and bring people to a mutual agreeable understanding. Set out each day to step up into the multitude of adverse situations and make earnest attempts to bring peace.

Prayer:

"Lord, may I step up in every adversarial situation and attempt to bring peace. I pray that Your Peace will govern my heart and mind today. With Your Help, I embrace myself to be a Reconciler today."

PATIENCE

Definition:

Patience is the ability to endure through unjust treatment because of your faith, and even go beyond the expected response to such attacks by acting in a non-retaliatory way.

Scriptures:

Matthew 5:10-12 (NIV) [10] **Blessed are those who are persecuted because of righteousness,** *for theirs is the kingdom of heaven.* **[11] "Blessed are you when people insult you, persecute you and falsely say all kinds of evil against you because of me.** *[12] Rejoice and be glad, because* **great is your reward in heaven**, *for in the same way they persecuted the prophets who were before you.*

Luke 6:22 (NIV) [22] **Blessed are you when men hate you, when they exclude you and insult you and reject your name as evil, because of the Son of Man.**

1 Peter 2:19-20 (NIV) [19] For **it is commendable if a man bears up under the pain of unjust suffering because he is conscious of God.** *[20] But how is it to your credit if you receive a beating for doing wrong and endure it? But if you suffer for doing good and you endure it, this is commendable before God.*

Matthew 5:38-42 (NIV 1984) An Eye for an Eye 38 "You have heard that it was said, 'Eye for eye, and tooth for tooth.' 39 But I tell you, Do not resist an evil person. **If someone strikes you on the right cheek, turn to him the other also.** *40 And if someone wants to sue you and take your tunic, let him have your cloak as well. 41 If someone forces you to go one mile,* **go with him two miles.** *42 Give to the one who asks you, and do not turn away from the one who wants to borrow from you.*

Matthew 16:24 (NIV 1984) 24 Then Jesus said to his disciples, "If anyone would come after me, **he must deny himself and take up his cross and follow me.**

Characteristic explained:

When Christ gave us the promise of the empowerment of the Holy Spirit in Acts 1 verse 8, He said that the Power of the Holy Spirit was for us to be His Witnesses. That word **"witnesses"** is the Greek word **"Martus"** which is akin to

"**Martur**" from which we derived our english word "**martyr.**" In essence, to be a witness is to approach everyday with the preparedness that you might be persecuted, slandered, receive unjust treatment, martyred, because of your allegiance and alignment with Christ. This value further defines us as children of God, of the Kingdom of Heaven. Jesus said that those who endure such treatment are blessed, and will receive a great reward in Heaven.

Life Application:

The life application of this characteristic really requires us to *"turn the other cheek"* and to *"walk the second mile."* We give full expression to this value when we willingly live a life of self-denial for the sake of Christ.

Prayer:

"Lord Jesus, May I, through the Power of Your Holy Spirit inside of me, be able to exhibit great patience and endurance today. May I put into practice what it means, and what You expect, for me to **"turn the other cheek"**, *to* **"walk the second mile"**, *and to* **"lend without expecting to receive it back.""**

EXAMPLE

Definition:

*B*eing an example is the expression we give as to how much we value the Lord Jesus, and the extent to which we desire to make His Name known among all people.

Scriptures:

Matthew 5:13-16 (NIV 1984) Salt and Light 13
*"**You are the salt of the earth**. But if the salt loses its saltiness, how can it be made salty again? It is no longer good for anything, except to be thrown out and trampled by men. 14 "**You are the light of the world**. A city on a hill cannot be hidden. 15 Neither do people light a lamp and put it under a bowl. Instead they put it on its stand, and it gives light to everyone in the house. 16 In the same way, **let your light shine before men, that they may see your good deeds and praise your Father in heaven**."*

*Matthew 12:34-37 (NIV 1984) 34 "You brood of vipers, how can you who are evil say anything good? For **out of the overflow of the heart the mouth speaks.** 35 **The good man brings good things out of the good stored up in him**, and the evil man brings evil things out of the evil stored up in him."*

1 Timothy 4:12 (NIV) [12] Don't let anyone look down on you because you are young, but **set an example for the believers** *in speech, in life, in love, in faith and* **in purity***.*

1 Corinthians 11:1 (NIV) "1 **Follow my example, as I follow the example of Christ.***"*

Characteristic explained:

Being an example is an inner awareness and aptitude to present oneself as an example to follow, which is visible through one's behaviour, actions and words.

Life Application:

Being an example is an intentional awareness that God made me a light to shine in such a way that it will bring and point people to Christ. Valuing being an Example is attending to one's conduct, and presenting oneself in the highest stature possible, at all times.

Prayer:

"Lord, I desire to make You Known to everyone I get in contact with today. By the Power that the Holy Spirit provides, I commit to be a good example for others to follow. May I be a light and Salt today, so that others will put their faith in You."

CUSTODIAN

Definition:

A custodian is someone who, not only intentionally obeys and keeps the Word of God, but protects and preserves the sanctity of it. A custodian is a keeper, preserver and defender of the Word of God and seeks in earnest to uphold the Word of God in every situation and circumstance. A custodian is intent on upholding the Word of God. A Custodian is an upholder, practitioner and advocate for the moral guidelines God set for His people.

Scriptures:

Matthew 5:19 (NIV 1984) "19 Anyone who breaks one of the least of these commandments and teaches others to do the same will be called least in the kingdom of heaven, but **whoever practices and teaches these commands will be called great in the kingdom of heaven.***"*

> *Mark 12:29-31 (NIV) 29* **"The most important one,"** *answered Jesus, "is this: 'Hear, O Israel: The Lord our God, the Lord is one.* **30 Love the Lord your God with all your heart and with all your soul and with all your mind and with all your strength.***' 31 The second is this: 'Love your neighbor as yourself.' There is no commandment greater than these."*

> *John 15:14 (NIV)* *"14 You are my friends* **if you do what I command.***"*

Characteristic explained:

To be a custodian is to keep something sacred and secured by intentional practice. To be a Custodian is to be a Law keeper. To be a custodian is to be a preserver of something that's of high value. Custodians are those people who live to keep valuable customs and principles, especially for future generations to observe. They are the protectors and good stewards of passing on the values and principles taught or passed on to them. A custodian is also one who guards and defends something of high value, from outside interference and influence.

Life Application:

From Jesus' teaching we learn that practicing and teaching people to obey the commandments of the Lord, is highly valued. We value being custodians when we both practice the observance of the Ten Commandments, as well as teach others to practice and obey it as well. As custodians of the commands of the Lord we firstly practice these commands in our own lives. The biggest impact we can ever make is by holding the commands of the Lord in observance in our own lives. When we keep these commands, we maintain the use of it, and thereby ensuring it's future use.

Prayer:

"Lord, I thank you for Your Word, and the Guidance it provides for me to live a Holy and Blessed Life. I will be a good Custodian of Your Word today by living it, practicing it, and applying it as my Moral Compass to every area and situation I face today."

RECONCILIATORY

Definition:

To be reconciliatory is to be a proactive initiator to restore relationships and defuse conflicts. We value reconciliation when we take the initiative to sort things out with a brother or sister, and this is what Jesus encourages us to do.

Scriptures:

> *Matthew 5:23-24 (NIV 1984) 23 "Therefore, **if you are offering your gift at the altar** and **there remember that your brother has something against you**, 24 leave your gift there in front of the altar. **First go and be reconciled to your brother**; then come and offer your gift.*

> *Matthew 18:15-17 (NIV 1984) **A Brother Who Sins Against You** 15 "If your brother sins against you, go and show him his fault, just*

> between the two of you. **If he listens to you, you have won your brother over.** 16 But if he will not listen, take one or two others along, so that 'every matter may be established by the testimony of two or three witnesses.' 17 If he refuses to listen to them, tell it to the church; and if he refuses to listen even to the church, treat him as you would a pagan or a tax collector.

> 2 Corinthians 5:18-20 (NIV) 18 All this is from God, who reconciled us to himself through Christ and gave us the ministry of reconciliation: 19 that God was reconciling the world to himself in Christ, not counting people's sins against them. And **he has committed to us the message of reconciliation.** 20 We are therefore Christ's ambassadors, as though God were making his appeal through us. We implore you on Christ's behalf: Be reconciled to God.

Characteristic explained:

Being a reconciler primarily is someone who desires and works towards restoring friendly relations with all people in their life. This applies to yourself when other people are upset with you, or have something against you, or with you assisting others to be reconciled, who have unsettled feuds between them. Reconciliation means that they settle their disputes appropriately and work together in unity and harmony going forward. Reconciliation requires humility, forgiveness, mercy and grace.

Life Application:

Many people have unsettled feuds. In humility, and in consistent pursuit of the instruction of the Lord to live at peace with all men, let us work out those feuds between ourselves. Let us also help our Brothers to resolve their broken relationships.

Prayer:

"Lord, I pray that I will have the courage to go to those whom I know have things against me, and to make an earnest attempt to be reconciled. Lord, I was reconciled to You, I pray that I will find reconciliation in all my relationships today."

RESOLUTENESS

Definition:

*R*esoluteness describes the value of being a man or woman of your word, even if when hurts.

Scriptures:

Matthew 5:37 (NIV 1984) 37 Simply **let your 'Yes' be 'Yes**,*' and your 'No,' 'No'; anything beyond this comes from the evil one.*

Matthew 5:33 (NIV) 33 "Again, you have heard that it was said to the people long ago, **'Do not break your oath, but fulfill to the Lord the vows you have made.***'*

Psalms 15:4 (NIV) "4 who despises a vile person, but honors those who fear the Lord; **who keeps an oath even when it hurts**, *and* **does not change their mind**;*"*

Deuteronomy 23:21 (NIV) 21 **If you make a vow to the Lord your God, do not be slow to pay it**, *for the Lord your God will certainly demand it of you and you will be guilty of sin.*

Joshua 24:15 "And if it seem evil unto you to serve the LORD, **choose you this day whom ye will serve***; whether the gods which your fathers served that were on the other side of the flood, or the gods of the Amorites, in whose land ye dwell: but as for me and my house, we will serve the LORD."*

Characteristic explained:

To be resolute is to make decisions firmly, purposefully, quickly and with determination. To be resolute is to make determined decisions. To be resolute is to not allow anything to get in the way of the decision you made. It is to be a man or woman of your word, and to stand by what you agreed, even if it hurts you. A resolute person is one that is solid, sound, firm, determined and unwavering to the oath or promise they made.

Life Application:

I grew up in South Africa, and I grew up on this value. We have a saying: *"My Word is my Bond."* It simply means that if I have given you my Word, it is as good as giving you a Bank Guaranteed Cheque. *Resolute people are unwavering in their convictions* and *decisive in fulfilling their word.* Be a person of your word!

Prayer:

"Lord, I pray that I will be a man/woman of my word today.

May I stand by my Biblically governed and Spirit-led decisions. May I be unwavering in fulfilling my promises since it reflects not only on me when I don't, but more importantly, on You. I want to please You in this matter Lord."

LOVING

Definition:

Love is a strong feeling of affection and endearment.

Scriptures:

Matthew 5:43-48 (NIV 1984) **Love for Enemies**
"43 "You have heard that it was said, 'Love your neighbor and hate your enemy.' 44 But I tell you: **Love your enemies and pray for those who persecute you, 45 that you may be sons of your Father in heaven***. He causes his sun to rise on the evil and the good, and sends rain on the righteous and the unrighteous. 46 If you love those who love you, what reward will you get? Are not even the tax collectors doing that? 47 And if you greet only your brothers, what are you doing more than others? Do not even pagans*

do that? 48 Be perfect, therefore, as your heavenly Father is perfect."

John 3:16 (NIV) **"For God so loved the world that He gave His One and Only Son;** *that whoever believes in Him will not perish but have eternal life."*

John 13:34 -35 (NIV) "34 A new commandment I give you: **Love one another. 35 By this everyone will know that you are my disciples, if you love one another."**

1 John 4:7-8 (NIV) "7 Dear friends, **let us love one another,** *for love comes from God. Everyone who loves has been born of God and knows God. 8 Whoever does not love does not know God, because* **God is love."**

1 John 4:12 (NIV) "No one has ever seen God; but **if we love one another, God lives in us** *and His love is made complete in us."*

Romans 12:10 (NIV) **"Be devoted to one another in brotherly love.** *Honor one another above yourselves."*

Characteristic explained:

Love can be explained by words such as affection, adoration, deep friendship, tenderness, fondness, amity and devotion. Love is that expression of tender affection towards somebody. Love is the affection you show when you like something or someone very much. Love is also when you feel a desire for somebody. Love is defined by a passionate attraction and desire towards someone. A strong liking and an accompanying friendly and kind enthusiasm express love.

Life Application:

We value loving when we give expression of our thoughts, through our heartfelt actions, to show and express endearment, adoration, affection, fondness and deep friendship. We value love when we unconditionally show our affection in meaningful ways. All people have a need and a desire to be loved.

Love is from God. Love God, love His people, love the Samaritans, and those who hurt, abused and rejected you. Love God's Commandments with all your heart. We show that we love God by the way we obey His commandments. Say to someone today: "*I love you!*" and mean it. Love drives away fear. Love unifies. There is power in love!

Prayer:

"Lord, I love you with all my heart, all my soul and all my strength. As a sign of my love and appreciation of You I will show your love to everyone around me today, even to my enemies and those whom I do not associate with usually. May I love people like You love me."

DISCREETNESS

Definition:

It is the inherent value of doing extra-ordinary things without desiring to be seen or even acknowledged for doing them, except as unto the Lord.

Scriptures:

Matthew 6:3-4 (NIV 1984) 3 But when you give to the needy, **do not let your left hand know what your right hand is doing***, 4 so that your giving may be in secret. Then your Father, who sees what is done in secret, will reward you.*

Matthew 6:6 (NIV) 6 But **when you pray***, go into your room,* **close the door and pray** *to your Father, who is unseen.* ***Then your Father, who sees what is done in secret, will reward you.***

Matthew 6:17-18 (NIV) 17 But **when you fast, put oil on your head** *and* **wash your face,** *18* **so that it will not be obvious to others that you are fasting,** *but only to your Father, who is unseen; and* **your Father, who sees what is done in secret, will reward you.**

Colossians 3:23-24 (NIV) 23 Whatever you do, work at it with all your heart, **as working for the Lord, not for human masters,** *24 since you know that you will receive an inheritance from* **the Lord as a reward.** *It is the Lord Christ you are serving.*

Characteristic explained:

Discreetness is to deeply value doing things to honour God, and not man. This is one of the most outstanding characteristics of Children of God, they practice discreetness. To be discreet is to do things in an inconspicuous, unnoticeable, and modest way. It is the value of doing things in secret. Discreetness is also to practice restraint in telling others all that you do and accomplish. It is to choose to rather understate achievements or things, than overstating them. It is the opposite of boastfulness.

Life Application:

I think that the Biblical teaching provide us with quite a significant example to follow. For us as Believers, we are sometimes called upon to exercise our faith in extra-ordinary ways, such as fasting. It is not the norm for people to fast, not even to fast for extended periods of time, however, for those of us who fast this is a value to embrace. As we observe the commands and leading of the Lord to give or fast for a cause, we need to take special caution to do so discreetly.

May the rewards from above, on our lives and ministry, tell that we pray. If indeed we do everything to honour God, then discreetness should be an easy value to embrace.

Prayer:

"Lord, may I be discreet in all that I do for You today. May I truly rely on Your reward for what I do and keep doing in secret for You. It is You that I want to please, not men. Whatever I do today, may I not do it to be seen by men, but truly, in a discreet way, to be seen by You."

FORGIVING

Definition:

Forgiveness is the ability to permanently release those who wronged you, and treat the offenders as if they never did a thing to hurt or harm you.

Scripture:

> *Matthew 6:12 (NIV 1984) 12 Forgive us our debts,* **as we also have forgiven our debtors.**

> *Matthew 6:14-15 (NIV 1984) 14 For* **if you forgive men when they sin against you, your heavenly Father will also forgive you.** *15 But if you do not forgive men their sins, your Father will not forgive your sins.*

> *Colossians 3:13 (NIV) "13* **Bear with each other and forgive one another** *if any of you has a grievance against someone.* **Forgive as the Lord forgave you.**"

> *Matthew 18:21-22 (NIV 1984) "21 Then Peter came to Jesus and asked, "Lord, **how many times shall I forgive my brother** when he sins against me? Up to seven times?" 22 Jesus answered, "I tell you, not seven times, but **seventy-seven times**."*

Characteristic explained:

Forgiveness is one of the strongest values on earth, but more specifically of the Christian Faith. Forgiveness holds the power to health and healing, but also to death and destruction. Forgiveness is defined by our ability to let go of an offence, hurt or wrong done to us.

It is that constant act of pardoning others. It is the extending of compassionate grace to those who hurt us, abuse us, and cause pain to us. Forgiveness is defined by being merciful, understanding, tolerant, and pitiful. It is in the light of our dependency and appreciation on God's forgiveness that we liberally forgive. The key to receiving and being forgiven is in our hands, therefor forgive.

Life Application

To be forgiving is to fill oneself with grace and mercy to forgive, every offence brought against you, before you leave your place of prayer every morning. What Jesus taught us was to forgive *"seventy seven times a day."* If the yardstick of **"seventy seven times seven"** is upheld in our lives, I believe that we will be a very forgiving people, and true examples of being followers of Jesus.

Even under extreme circumstances do we find the example of Jesus and His Disciples bearing witness of this value in their lives. The words: *"Father forgive them, for they do not know what they are doing,"* stand as a testimony and an example for us to follow.

May we forgive often, willingly and freely. I am reminded of this value in my life every morning when I bow down to pray and recite the *"**Our Father.**"* May this prayer, especially the *"**and forgive us our trespasses as we forgive those who trespassed against us,**"* find a permanent home in our actions and dealings with others everyday. May our attitudes and actions bear witness of our heartfelt pardoning of others.

Prayer:

"Lord, please forgive me as I forgive those who have sinned against me. May I be prepared, and full of grace to forgive every offence and sin done to and against me today."

KINGDOM OF GOD INVESTOR

Definition:

A Kingdom of God Investor is someone who values the Kingdom of God above earthly thing and as an expression of that value, puts his or her treasures into the Kingdom of God.

Scriptures:

Matthew 6:19-21 (NIV 1984) Treasures in Heaven
"19 "Do not store up for yourselves treasures on earth, where moth and rust destroy, and where thieves break in and steal. 20 But **store up for yourselves treasures in heaven***, where moth and rust do not destroy, and where thieves do not break in and steal. 21* **For where your treasure is, there your heart will be also.***"*

Acts 2:44-45 (NIV) "*44 All **the believers** were together and **had everything in common**. 45 **They sold property and possessions to give to anyone who had need**.*"

*Acts 4:32 (NIV) **The Believers Share Their Possessions** "32 All the believers were one in heart and mind. **No one claimed that any of their possessions was their own, but they shared everything they had**.*"

---

*2 Corinthians 9:6 (NIV) Generosity Encouraged "6 Remember this: Whoever sows sparingly will also reap sparingly, and **whoever sows generously will also reap generously**.*"

*2 Corinthians 9:7-8 (NIV) 7 Each of you should give what you have decided in your heart to give, not reluctantly or under compulsion, for **God loves a cheerful giver**. 8 And **God is able to bless you abundantly**, so that in all things at all times, having all that you need, you will abound in every good work.*

*2 Corinthians 9:10-11 (NIV) 10 Now **he who supplies seed to the sower and bread for food will also supply and increase your store of seed** and will enlarge the harvest of your righteousness. 11 **You will be enriched in every way so that you can be generous on every occasion**, and through us your generosity will result in thanksgiving to God.*

Characteristic explained:

The Principle of sowing and reaping stand central in this value. *Whatever we sow, we reap.* The best place to sow is in the Kingdom of God. The early **Believers truly valued the Teachings of the Lord Jesus** by not storing for themselves treasures on earth. Their treasures were sown into the Kingdom of God, and therefor, as the Scriptures say: *"their heart would be there also."* It never ceases to amaze me to see where people's hearts are, and how they value the Kingdom of God in relation to how they treasure it with their treasures.

Over the last few years I've seen so many properties being given to us to advance the work of planting new churches, and all of them from developing Nations. I've see so many poor people, who do not even own their own car or home, willingly give up their family land so that another church could be built. Investments made into the work of God should reflect how we value God's work, and how we value being entrusted with seed.

Life Application:

To value the Kingdom of God is to treasure it. We treasure the Kingdom of God when we place our proceeds with a willing and cheerful heart into the local Church and into advancing the Kingdom of God in the Nations.

How do we do that? 1. We honour God with a tithe (ten percent) of all our income; 2. We offer up to Him a sacrificial gift from the remaining ninety percent of our income, just as we obediently and willingly present to our Governments that part of our income as tax, as what they require of us to give. 3. We sow into the Work of God by supporting Missionaries, Orphanages, the destitute and the poor. The latter should be done in secret and not done so that others could see.

You might ask: **"So what can we live from?"** In fact, if we keep the Biblical Principle of *"owing no man anything"* then we will actually have enough to live a good life. Without debt most people can live a reasonable living compared to their income. **How do we get there?** Start reducing those things that are nice to have but deprive you of putting your treasure in the house of God. **It is better to live in favour with God than be admired by man.** Save and only buy what you can afford. Be a Kingdom of God Investor, showing yourself to value the teachings and Words of Jesus above that of the society we live in.

Prayer:

"Lord Jesus, I pray that I will be a good steward of the resources you have entrusted to me. May the way I use what You gave me reflect that I Treasure You more than anything on earth."

GOD-MINDED

Definition:

*B*eing God-minded means that you think about God, His Word and the eternal things of above, all the time. It is a Kingdom value to be God-minded.

Scripture:

Matthew 6:24 (NIV 1984) 24 "No one can serve two masters. Either he will hate the one and love the other, or he will be devoted to the one and despise the other. **You cannot serve both God and Money**.

Colossians 3:1-2 (NIV) 1 Since, then, you have been raised with Christ, **set your hearts on things above**, where Christ is, seated at the right hand of God. 2 **Set your minds on things above**, not on earthly things.

Romans 8:5 (NIV) "5 Those who live according to the flesh have their minds set on what the flesh desires; but those who **live in accordance with the Spirit have their minds set on what the Spirit desires.***"*

Psalms 1:2 (NIV) "2 but whose delight is in the law of the Lord, and **who meditates on his law day and night.***"*

Deuteronomy 6:4-9 (NIV) 4 Hear, O Israel: The Lord our God, the Lord is one. 5 **Love the Lord your God with all your heart and with all your soul and with all your strength.** *6 These commandments that I give you today are to be on your hearts. 7 Impress them on your children. Talk about them when you sit at home and when you walk along the road, when you lie down and when you get up. 8 Tie them as symbols on your hands and bind them on your foreheads. 9 Write them on the door frames of your houses and on your gates.*

Characteristic explained:

To be God-minded is to be single-minded on God, and the things of God. From the earliest dealings with man, God always expressed a desire and commanded that *He should be at the centre of our thoughts, actions and deliberations*. He encouraged His people to love Him with all of their hearts, mind and strength. He wanted His people to talk about Him all the time, and to make permanent reminders to carry with them. He also encouraged His people to write His commandments on the doorposts of their houses. To be God-minded is to take every effort and action to keep the Lord God at the forefront of our thought, action and speech.

Life Application:

How do we put this Kingdom Value into action in our lives? Well, a good way to do that is to start each day by reading and meditating on the Word of God, and to pray. When I was a child we used to **learn memory verses** for school and Sunday school. This might be a good discipline to practice, now that we are older and our capacity much more increased, to **learn one of the verses we read during our morning devotion** and then to **recite them to our families** during our evening family devotion. This way we will both meditate on the Word of God, and keep the Word of God at the forefront of our minds.

Another, more permanent way might be to **put meaningful Scriptures up on our walls as statement or art pieces, but also as declaration Scriptures**. I grew up during a time when many of the picture frames in my Grandparents' houses were Scriptures, or parts thereof. It served as a constant reminder of who they served. The more I think about it, the more I see the incredible value that was to them and their children, and even to us as youngsters. We live in a different era and maybe we could put Scriptures up as a screensavers or as background pictures on our smart watches, smartphones, tablets and computers.

The goal is not just to place outward signs, but to **create ways in which we can be more God-minded in our every day life**. I pray that you too will set up such signposts for your life to keep the Lord God at the centre of your life.

Prayer:

"Lord, I pray that Your Word will be at the forefront of my mind every day. Give me the courage to speak about Your Word more often, especially in my house. Lord, I commit to think on You and Your Word more!"

KINGDOM OF GOD PRIORITIZER

Definition:

We truly value the Kingdom of God when we seek to put the Kingdom values above that of our own. We value the Kingdom of God when it takes precedence over every decision we make.

Scripture:

Matthew 6:33 (NIV 1984) 33 But **seek first his kingdom and his righteousness**, *and all these things will be given to you as well.*

2 Chronicles 18:4 (NIV) 4 But Jehoshaphat also said to the king of Israel, "**First seek the counsel of the Lord.**"

Matthew 6:10-13 (NIV) 10 **your kingdom come, your will be done**, *on earth as it is in heaven. 11 Give us today our daily bread. 12 And forgive us our debts, as we also have forgiven our debtors. 13 And lead us not into temptation, but deliver us from the evil one.*

Colossians 3:15 (AMPC) 15 And **let the peace** *(soul harmony which comes)* **from Christ rule** *(act as umpire continually)* **in your hearts** *[deciding and* **settling with finality all questions that arise in your minds**, *in that peaceful state] to which as [members of Christ's] one body you were also called [to live]. And be thankful (appreciative), [giving praise to God always].*

Characteristic explained:

A KINGDOM of God seeker prioritizes the Will of God over his or her own. **To have this as a Value in one's life means that you seek guidance, approval, direction and favour from God prior to doing anything.** It is that heartfelt submission to the Will of God in everything we do. Before we decide on anything, we seek what God wants us to do in regards to that matter. It requires the daily desire to walk in the perfect will of God.

Life Application:

We value being a Kingdom of God seeker when we **intentionally seek God's approval, guidance, and instruction prior to doing anything.** It is that daily enquiring of the Lord for His Will to be done. It is to submit every decision to God for His guidance and ultimate instruction.

. . .

PEACE PLAYS a major part in knowing assuredly what the will of God is in any decision.

I remember that my Dad taught us this value. He never made any big decision without first submitting such decision to prayer and guidance from the Lord. Sometimes the answer was yes, and other times it was no, but I saw how they submitted to the Will of God in every decision. They sought Him first and settled with His guidance on it. This was in relation to decisions like changing a job, buying a new car, a house, or going on holiday. Sometimes without even asking, my Parents would sense that the Lord led them to give or sow into a matter. They also sometimes felt the guidance to fast and pray for a season. Whatever the Lord directed them to do is what they did. This is the pattern I followed in my life.

How do we do this? Submit your decisions to God in prayer, and then over coming days, as you read His Word, or listen to the inner voice of the Holy Spirit, find His guidance. You will always have a strong sense of peace when you've conceded to the Will of God.

Prayer:

"Heavenly Father, I come to You in prayer today to commit myself to You and to doing Your Will daily. Lord, help me to seek You first in every decision I have to make today. Holy Spirit help me in seeking the Will of God first, but also to commit myself to doing it and following through by doing what please You most."

INTROSPECTIVE

Definition:

It is the constant self-awareness and assessment of our own standing before God, and thereby enabling us to be considered in our assessment of others' actions and deeds.

Scripture:

Matthew 7:1-2 (NIV 1984) 1 "**Do not judge, or you too will be judged. 2 For in the same way you judge others, you will be judged,** and with the measure you use, it will be measured to you.

Matthew 7:3-5 (NIV) 3 "**Why do you look at the speck of sawdust in your brother's eye and pay no attention to the plank in your own eye?** 4 How can you say to your brother, 'Let me take the speck out of your eye,' when all the time *there is a plank in your own eye? 5 You hypocrite,* **first take the plank out of your own eye, and then you will see clearly to remove the speck from your brother's eye.***"*

John 8:7 (NIV) "7 When they kept on questioning him, he straightened up and said to them, **"Let any one of you who is without sin be the first to throw a stone at her.***""*

Characteristic explained:

To value being introspective is valuing first assessing one's own life before passing comment or judgement on others. **Introspection helps us make balanced assessments of other's actions.** Being introspective is being thoughtful, reflective and considered in one's approach to others. It is the embracing of that self-examining, contemplative approach to everyday life.

Life Application:

THE QUESTION that helps us being level-headed in every situation is always: *"If others had to assess me in the matter of my concern or judgement, what would they say?"* If there might even be the slightest chance that they would judge my actions, behaviour or manners in the same way, then maybe I should not be the one to pass judgement. Jesus demonstrated this with the woman who was caught in adultery. I wonder how much more gracious we would live towards others if we truly value introspection. May we always be introspective before passing comments or judgements on others.

Prayer:

"Lord, search my heart today and see if there be any way in me that is offensive and that has the potential of driving people away from You? Lord, help me to deal with these faults and shortcomings of mine before I even look or think of passing judgement on others. Have mercy on me oh God!"

PERSISTENCE

Definition:

*B*eing persistent is living a life in full pursuit without giving up. Keep on asking, seeking and knocking since we have this Promise. Persistence moves you to explore every possibility for an outcome.

Scriptures:

Matthew 7:7-8 (NIV 1984) "7 "**Ask** *and it will be given to you;* **seek** *and you will find;* **knock** *and the door will be opened to you.* **8 For everyone who asks receives; he who seeks finds; and to him who knocks, the door will be opened.**"

Luke 18:1 (NIV) The Parable of the Persistent Widow "1 Then **Jesus told his disciples** *a parable to show them that* **they should always pray and not give up.**"

Romans 2:7 (NIV) "To those who by persistence in doing good seek glory, honor and immortality, he will give eternal life.'

Characteristic explained:

Persistence is the value of being persevering, tenacious, enduring and unrelenting. It is in inner aptitude of hope and faith that things will come through, things will turn out ok, that circumstances will change for good. Persistence is seen in the way one shows determination and obstinacy to not give in or give up. Through the Parable of the Persistent Woman, Jesus taught us this lesson of persistent pursuit of the things we believe in, and to trust the Lord to do things in our lives, without wavering.

Life Application:

We all have hopes and dreams, unfortunately many of us give up on our hopes and dreams as if they are unreachable. We apply this value in our lives when we start hoping and dreaming again. Start believing again that the impossible can become possible. When you trust God for something, don't give up on holding on to that Promise, that Scripture, or that Message from God. Hold on to promises of God like Joseph who believed God, and saw the fulfillment of God's Promise to him. He was persistent and saw the fulfillment of the dream God gave him. Be like an Abraham who believed God, even though he and his wife were as good as dead.

Prayer:

"Lord, with the help Your Holy Spirit provides, I will not give in or give up pursuing fulfilling the tasks You set before me. By Faith in You and in Your Word I am holding on to Your Promises. I

*pray that You will find in me that **"Persistent Woman"** You referred to in the Parable."*

CONSIDERATION

Definition:

*C*onsideration is the value of **acting thoughtfully** and **with careful consideration**, beforehand, as to how your preferences, actions, presence at certain places and responses, might impact others.

Scriptures:

Matthew 7:12 (NIV 1984) 12 So in everything, **do to others what you would have them do to you,** *for this sums up the Law and the Prophets.*

Philippians 2:4 **"Look not every man on his own things***, but every man also on the things of others."*

Romans 14:13 (NIV) "13 Therefore let us stop passing judgment on one another. Instead, **make up your mind not to put any stumbling block or obstacle in the way of a brother or sister.***"*

Characteristic explained:

BEING CONSIDERATE IS BEING THOUGHTFUL, mindful, and careful about how one's actions and words might negatively impact others. To be considerate is to be mindful, respectful, selfless and kind, especially as it relates to others. Consideration is applied when we consciously think about our actions, words and reactions beforehand. To be considerate is to be contemplative, understanding and sympathetic.

Life Application:

We are considerate when we act in a thoughtful and mindful way towards others. We are considerate when we honestly assess our reactions and responses, beforehand, to ensure that they will not impact others negatively. The question: *"Would I like others to treat me in the way in which I am about to treat someone else?"* The answer to this question should answer and show us just how considerate we really are. So, on the one hand "Consideration" is the application and thoughtfulness over How our conduct, liberties and presence might negatively impact others, but then also how considered we are in treating people with the same kind of respect and courtesy as what we would love them to treat us.

Prayer:

"Lord Jesus, may the Words of my mouth and the meditation of my heart be acceptable in Your sight. Lord, May I be considerate in the way I live and respond to others today.

May there be no selfish or self-seeking way that obstructs others to see You in me. May I apply care in treating others in the way I would like to be treated."

CONSERVATIVE

Definition:

To be conservative is the considered choice of living rather carefully than liberally. It is the making of careful and conservative choices within the guidelines of the Bible. You would rather err on being too conservative than allowing yourself liberties that might be frowned upon by God, and then also by others.

Scriptures:

Matthew 7:13-14 (NIV 1984) "13 "**Enter through the narrow gate.** *For wide is the gate and broad is the road that leads to destruction, and many enter through it. 14 But* **small is the gate and narrow the road that leads to life,** *and only a few find it."*

Matthew 5:28-30 (NIV) 28 But I tell you that anyone who looks at a woman lustfully has already committed adultery with her in his heart. 29 If your right eye causes you to stumble, gouge it out and throw it away. It is better for you to lose one part of your body than for your whole body to be thrown into hell. 30 And if your right hand causes you to stumble, cut it off and throw it away. **It is better for you to lose one part of your body than for your whole body to go into hell.**

1 Corinthians 10:23-24 (NIV) "23 **"I have the right to do anything,"** *you say—* **but not everything is beneficial.** *"I have the right to do anything"—* **but not everything is constructive.** *24* **No one should seek their own good, but the good of others."**

1 Corinthians 10:31-33 (NIV) "31 **So whether you eat or drink or whatever you do,** *do it all for the glory of God. 32* **Do not cause anyone to stumble**, *whether Jews, Greeks or the church of God— 33 even as I try to please everyone in every way.* **For I am not seeking my own good but the good of many, so that they may be saved."**

Colossians 3:17 (NIV) "17 And **whatever you do, whether in word or deed, do it all in the name of the Lord Jesus,** *giving thanks to God the Father through him."*

Characteristic explained:

THE BIBLE IS the Handbook on conservative and considered living. When we consider the many laws and commandments God gave His people, we observe that they are rules and guidelines for conservative and considered living. Firstly, we apply the Word of God to our actions and reactions, and then we consider the way it might impact others, and then we also consider how others might view our behaviour, but most of all, how God would view my behaviour.

Life Application:

The Scriptures we explored on Conservative living, to name a few, direct our attention to make decisions more on the conservative side than on the liberal side of life. Scripture clearly teaches us to be considered in our liberties, especially as it might negatively affect or impact a weaker person in their faith. I pray that God will help us value being "Conservative" more than being seen as liberal, broad-minded and "with it." It is a Value in the Kingdom of God to be intentionally more conservative than liberal.

Prayer:

"Lord Jesus, help me to do whatever would please You most and be in alignment with what Your Word teaches me. I would rather be in right standing with You than do things, or take up some liberties and bring Your Good Name into disrepute. My desire is to please You more!"

FRUIT-BEARING

Definition:

To be *"fruit bearing"* is to both exhibit the change Christ brought into one's own life as well as bearing fruit through successfully leading others to follow Christ as well. Fruit-bearing is neither the one nor the other, it is both simultaneous, consistent and enduring.

Scriptures:

Matthew 7:16-18 (NIV 1984) 16 **By their fruit you will recognize them.** *Do people pick grapes from thornbushes, or figs from thistles? 17 Likewise* **every good tree bears good fruit**, *but a bad tree bears bad fruit. 18 A good tree cannot bear bad fruit, and a bad tree cannot bear good fruit.*

Matthew 12:33 (NIV 1984) 33 "**Make a tree good and its fruit will be good**, *or make a tree bad and its fruit will be bad, for a tree is recognized by its fruit.*

Matthew 13:23 (NIV 1984) 23 But the one who received the seed that fell on good soil is the man who hears the word and understands it. **He produces a crop, yielding a hundred, sixty or thirty times what was sown.**"

Matthew 21:43 (NIV 1984) 43 "Therefore I tell you that the kingdom of God will be taken away from you and **given to a people who will produce its fruit.**"

John 15:5 & 8 (NIV) "I am the vine; you are the branches. **If you remain in me and I in you, you will bear much fruit;** *apart from me you can do nothing. 8* **This is to my Father's glory, that you bear much fruit, showing yourselves to be my disciples.**"

Characteristic explained:

One of the most powerful ways in which we show and proof our legitimacy as Children of God, who turned from our wicked ways unto the living God, is to bear the fruit of a changed life in our lives. It is also the ability to reproduce after our own, renewed, self. We can tell people all we want, but what they really look at and hear is what we model with our lives. Fruit-bearing is one of the signs that we are truly Disciples.

Life Application:

THE BEST WAY TO apply this Kingdom Value is by daily considering the miracle of salvation, and being born again. When we consider the work of God in us, we can't but be filled with a deep appreciation of His wondrous recreative and renewal work. This daily reminder should inspire us to live close to the renewed Nature of God in us. When we are born again we become one in spirit with God. We are born of the Holy Spirit. It is the nature of the Holy Spirit in us that should be lived and seen by everyone around us. If He directs and reigns supremely, then He will bring forth everlasting fruit in us. Make it your life ambition to be a bearer of Good fruit.

Prayer:

"Dear Lord, may my life bear the fruit of the change You brought in me. Father, may I bring you glory by bearing good fruit with the life I live. May I be a fruitful branch in Your Vine, bearing lasting fruit. Father God, prune every part of my branch that does not bear fruit, that I may be a more fruit-producing branch in You. Make me Fruitful and let me multiply."

PRACTITIONER

Definition:

We show that we value the Kingdom of God by being doers of the Word. Jesus values doers, those putting things He teaches into practice in their lives. It is a value in the Kingdom of God to be a practitioner.

Scriptures:

*Matthew 7:24 (NIV 1984) The Wise and Foolish Builders "24 "Therefore **everyone who hears these words of mine** and **puts them into practice** is like a wise man who built his house on the rock."*

*John 14:23 (NIV) "23 Jesus replied, "**Anyone who loves me will obey my teaching.** My Father will love them, and we will come to them and make our home with them."*

James 1:22 (NIV) "22 Do not merely listen to the word, and so deceive yourselves. **Do what it says.***"*

Romans 2:13 (NIV) "13 For it is not those who hear the law who are righteous in God's sight, but it is **those who obey the law who will be declared righteous.***"*

Luke 6:47-49 (NIV) 47 As for **everyone who comes to me and hears my words and puts them into practice**, *I will show you what they are like. 48 They are like a man building a house, who dug down deep and laid the foundation on rock. When a flood came, the torrent struck that house but could not shake it, because it was well built. 49 But the one who hears my words and does not put them into practice is like a man who built a house on the ground without a foundation. The moment the torrent struck that house, it collapsed and its destruction was complete."*

Luke 8:21 (NIV) "21 He replied, "My mother and brothers **are those who hear God's word and put it into practice.***"*

Philippians 4:9 (NIV) "9 Whatever you have learned or received or heard from me, or seen in me — **put it into practice.** *And the God of peace will be with you."*

Characteristic explained:

The way Jesus taught us, we can't but apply this value to our lives. Who doesn't want to be seen as a wise man?

Who of us want to be seen to be a fool? None of us want to be seen to be foolish. This value places a high premium on doing and applying the teachings of Jesus, against simply just hearing it, talking about it or telling others to do it.

Life Application:

We value being a practitioner when we daily consider how we may put the Word of God, from our morning devotions, into practice in our lives. God loves doers. The Lord delights in those who put His words into practice. Take time every morning to consider how you will put His Teachings into practice. Think of ways in which you can apply His teachings to the way you speak, the things you do or actions you could take in certain situations in which you could and should take action. We show our love to Christ when we do whatever He asks of us. Obedience is seen in how we put the teachings of Jesus into practice.

Prayer:

"Father, this is my prayer and desire that I put into practice everything You taught us. I want to honor You by putting Your Teachings into practice. According to Your Word I desire to show You how much I love You by doing everything You demand from me."

ACCOUNTABILITY

Definition:

Accountability is to value of living answerable for one's actions, deeds and words, both to man and God. **Accountability is expressed by taking responsibility** for one's actions and words.

Scripture:

Matthew 12:36 (NIV) 12 " But **I tell you that men will have to give account on the day of judgement for every careless word they have spoken.**"

Romans 14:12 (NIV) "12 So then, **each of us will give an account of ourselves to God.**"

Hebrews 4:13 (NIV) "13 **Nothing in all creation is hidden from God**'s *sight. Everything is uncovered and laid bare before the eyes of him* **to whom we must give account.**"

1 Peter 4:5 (NIV) "5 *But* **they will have to give account to him who is ready to judge the living and the dead.**"

Colossians 4:6 (NIV) "6 *Let your conversation be always full of grace, seasoned with salt,* **so that you may know how to answer everyone.**"

Characteristic explained:

Accountability is **one of the essential qualities of a mature person.** Accountability is to take responsibility for one's actions. Being accountable means that one is answerable, and takes responsibility and liable.

Life Application:

God desires that we live answerable for whatever we do. Making decisions based on the fact that you take liability for what you say and do shows that you have become accountable. It is easy to pass the buck or shift the blame when things go wrong, however, **it is a Value in the Kingdom of God to take responsibility** and assume liability when it is needed.

Many people live a life in denial or blaming others for everything that happens in their lives. They blame others for their actions, behaviour and the way they respond, but God desires that we live answerable for our own actions, not just to others, but also as it relates to God.

Prayer:

"Lord, I take full responsibility for my actions and words today. I pray that with the help of the Holy Spirit that I will apply greater care to live accountable to You and those to whom I give account on earth. Father, may I live in such a way that whenever people ask me about the hope I have in my heart that I will be able to answer them without shame as to the Hope that You are in my life."

LIVING BY FAITH

Definition:

*F*aith believes beyond proof. Faith is doing things because of what you belief to be true. Faith is acting purely because God said you should or could. Our actions flow from what we truly belief.

Scriptures:

*Mark 11:22 (NIV) "22 **Have faith in God**," Jesus answered."*

Matthew 17:20 (NIV 1984) 20 He replied, "Because you have so little faith. I tell you the truth, **if you have faith as small as a mustard seed,** *you can say to this mountain, 'Move from here to there' and it will move. Nothing will be impossible for you.'"*

Acts 20:21 (NIV) "21 I have declared to both Jews and Greeks that **they must turn to God** in repentance and **have faith in our Lord Jesus.**"

Romans 1:17 (NIV 1984) 17 For in the gospel a righteousness from God is revealed, **a righteousness that is by faith** *from first to last, just as it is written:* "**The righteous will live by faith.**"

Hebrews 11:1 (NIV) Faith in Action "1 Now **faith is confidence in what we hope for** and assurance about what we do not see."

Characteristic explained:

Having Faith is that ability to live with hope, assurance and trust that the future is good and that everything will work out. **Having faith is that confident reliance in someone or something. Faith is to have strong conviction in what you belief.** Faith is expressed and seen by our loyalty, commitment and devotion.

Life Application:

As Believers, we give expression to the strong faith and believe we have in the Triune God, that we undergird every situation with hope and assurance that God is in control and that His Will will be done. As Believers we give expression to our faith by our loyal commitment and devotion to the teachings of Christ. Believers are loyal people. We are people whom people can trust and rely on. We are positive and express our assurance in the Almighty God's Sovereignty in everything that we might face and go through. We are always hopeful, faithful, reliant, committed, and loyal. Believers are faith-filled people.

Prayer:

"Lord, I have put my faith in You. My prayer today is that the faith I have in You will be visible and that others will be drawn to also put their faith in You. Lord, I live by faith in You!"

CHILDLIKENESS

Definition:

*C*hildlikeness is the heart attitude of humility towards God, expressed by simple obedience in action. Those who value childlikeness take the Words of the Lord Jesus literally and apply it without trying to dissect or interpret it. They simply do what is asked.

Scripture:

*Matthew 18:3-5 (NIV 1984) 3 And he said: "I tell you the truth, **unless you change and become like little children,** you will never enter the kingdom of heaven. 4 Therefore, **whoever humbles himself like this child is the greatest in the kingdom of heaven.** 5 "And whoever welcomes a little child like this in my name welcomes me.*

Characteristic explained:

This value is characterized by simple faith, obedience and childlikeness. Jesus explained this value by defining what it requires. He defined that it requires humility to enter the Kingdom of God. Jesus came to teach us about the Kingdom of Heaven. Whenever you hear the word "**Kingdom**," you have a King and His Kingdom. No democratically determined, popularized ideas are welcomed in the Kingdom of God. **It takes simple faith and trust to belief that whatever Jesus taught was well considered and has** as a predetermined outcome, **our best interest at heart**. Childlikeness determines to trust the Lord's judgment and determination as final and conclusive.

Life Application:

We act and value childlikeness when we apply simple faith and trust to put the words of Jesus into practice in our lives. It never ceases to amaze me how strong certain cultures are around the world, simply for applying childlike faith to their daily living. The greatest advancement of the Gospel appears among those who are still moved by the simple instructions of the Lord. They act and do without questioning or doubting the Lord's guidance and instruction.

I dare to say that the opposite of Childlikeness is unbelief and doubt. *As and when the Lord instructs you to do things, act on it without reservation, this I deem to be childlikeness.*

Noah built and Ark, and **Moses acted in childlike faith** to walk into a flooding river to see it part for the Israelites to pass through on dry ground. He acted in childlike faith to strike a rock to provide water for the people of God in the desert. The young prophets acted with childlike faith to cut a stick and throw it into the water to become sweet. The Widow acted in childlike faith to gather all her neighbors' jars to pour oil into it from the little she had. It is this childlike faith which was seen in the Apostles when they laid their hands on the sick and saw them recover. The Apostle Paul acted on it when he grabbed a poisonous snake and nothing happened to him when the snake bit him. He simply acted in childlike faith to what Jesus said in Mark 16:18 (NIV).

> *Mark 16:18 (NIV)* "*18* **they will pick up snakes with their hands;** *and when they drink deadly poison,* **it will not hurt them at all;** *they will place their hands on sick people, and they will get well."*

CHILDLIKE FAITH IS what I grew up on. My Dad quoted Mark 16:18 every time he prayed for us when we were unwell. He practised Childlike faith and we had childlike faith to believe that what the Bible said was true and we embraced our healing since Dad acted on the Word of God. Let us be those who add this value of the Kingdom of God to our lives.

Prayer:

"Father God, may I walk with childlike faith today, to do whatever You ask me to do without questioning You. Father, may my simple obedience bring honor to You and to Your Name."

UNITY

Definition:

Unity is expressed by a heart attitude that desires to work together with others and seek to find mutual agreement and cooperation for the sake of Christ.

Scriptures:

*Matthew 18:19 (NIV 1984) 19 "Again, I tell you that **if two of you on earth agree about anything you ask for,** it **will be done for you** by my Father in heaven.*

*John 21:20-23 (NIV) "20 "My prayer is not for them alone. **I pray also for those who will believe in me** through their message, **21 that all of them may be one, Father, just as you are in me and I am in you.** May they also be in us so **that the world may believe that you have*** *sent me. 22 I have given them the glory that you gave me,* **that they may be one as we are one — 23 I in them and you in me — so that they may be brought to complete unity.** *Then the world will know that you sent me and have loved them even as you have loved me."*

Acts 4:32 (NIV) "**32 All the believers were one in heart and mind.** *No one claimed that any of their possessions was their own, but they shared everything they had."*

1 Corinthians 1:10 (NIV) "10 **I appeal to you**, *brothers and sisters, in the name of our Lord Jesus Christ,* **that all of you agree with one another** *in what you say and that there be no divisions among you, but that you* **be perfectly united in mind and thought**."

Psalms 133:1 and 3 (NIV) "**1 How good and pleasant it is when God's people live together in unity!** *3 It is as if the dew of Hermon were falling on Mount Zion.* **For there the Lord bestows his blessing, even life forevermore**."

Amos 3:3 (NIV) "*3 Do two walk together* **unless they have agreed to do so?**"

Characteristic explained:

One another statements are frequent throughout the New Testament. God desires His children to live at peace and in agreement with one another. The Lord desires that we are **ONE**. The Lord desires that **through us living in unity and agreement** with one another, that **people will belief and put**

their faith in God. Unity, cooperation and agreement lies at the heart of those who belong to the Kingdom of God. It stems from our own humility to advance the purposes and desires of our King. The very heart of our relationship with the Triune God is set in agreement through the covenant relationship we entered into through the Blood of Jesus. Unity is defined for us by our covenant relationship with God, Every time we partake of the Table of the Lord, we affirm our agreement, our covenant relationship with God.

Life Application:

WE ARE the Body of Christ and **Unity is vitally important** to our health and sustenance. As an expression of our covenant relationship with God through the shed Blood of Jesus, we always work towards the best interest of our mutually bound covenant partners. We live in an era where individualism is prized, however, in the Kingdom of God we prize and value agreement and unity. **It is such a stark value to observe when people put away their own wants and preferences to work towards that which build collaboration and unity.**

Unity is what God desires. As Children of God we show our Kingdom Values when we openly put away our own preferences in favor of that which will bring agreement and unity. Take steps every day to work together with others. Harness yourself to set aside your wants and desires and to be willing to build unity wherever you work. The level of unity determines the level of impact we have in this world. God commands His blessing where there is unity and agreement.

Prayer:

"Lord, I pray for unity among Your people. Start with me. I

pray that You will have in me a Unity Builder. I pray that through the Power of Your Holy Spirit that I will be working towards what brings Unity and agreement among Your people. Make us One Lord, that the world will know that You live in me, and that they will put their trust in You."

SERVANTHOOD

Definition:

Servanthood is the value of serving and helping others for their benefit and good.

Scriptures:

Matthew 20:26-28 (NIV 1984) "26 Not so with you. Instead, **whoever wants to become great among you must be your servant,** *27 and* **whoever wants to be first must be your slave**— *28 just as the Son of Man did not come to be served, but to serve, and to give his life as a ransom for many."*

Ephesians 6:7-8 (NIV) **Serve wholeheartedly,** *as* **if you were serving the Lord, not people,** *8 because you know that* **the Lord will reward each one** *for whatever good they do, whether they are slave or free.*

Colossians 3:23-24 (NIV) "*3 Whatever you do, work at it with all your heart, as working for the Lord, not for human masters, 24 since you know that you will receive an inheritance from the Lord as a reward.* **It is the Lord Christ you are serving.**"

Romans 12:11 (NIV) "*11 Never be lacking in zeal, but* **keep your spiritual fervor, serving the Lord.**"

1 Peter 4:10 (NIV) "*10* **Each of you should** *use whatever gift you have received to* **serve others**, *as faithful stewards of God's grace in its various forms.*"

Galatians 5:13 (NIV) "*13 You, my brothers and sisters, were called to be free. But do not use your freedom to indulge the flesh; rather,* **serve one another humbly in love.**"

Characteristic explained:

Servanthood is the practice from an internal value and willingness to helping others. Being a servant requires humility, and an ability to give yourself to the benefit of others. Servanthood is at the top of the values defining Great Leaders in the Kingdom of God. Great Leaders in the Kingdom of God are characterized by their serving.

Life Application:

We value Servanthood when we go out of our way to help others. It is the selfless act of stepping into a situation to assist others with something they need help with. We need to do so wholeheartedly, with love, diligently, not just please men but to please God. Seek opportunities each day to serve others.

Prayer:

"Lord, I pray that You will find in me a willing servant to do Your Will. May I truly be Your Hands and Feet. May I serve Your people with the gifts and skills You have given me, to build them up and to bring encouragement and hope. I am Your Servant willing to do whatever Yu desire me to do today."

LOYALTY

Definition:

To be **Loyal** is to be committed. Loyalty is the allegiance one commits to.

Scriptures:

Luke 9:62 (KJV) "[62] And Jesus said unto him, **No man, having put his hand to the plough, and looking back, is fit for the kingdom of God.**"

Psalm 37:5 "**Commit thy way unto the LORD; trust also in him;** and he shall bring it to pass."

1 Samuel 22:14 (NIV) "Ahimelek answered the king, "**Who of all your servants is as loyal as David,** the king's son-in-law, captain of your bodyguard and highly respected in your household?"

*Psalms 12:1 (NIV) "**1 Help, Lord, for no one is faithful anymore; those who are loyal have vanished from the human race.**"*

*John 15:13 "Greater love hath no man than this, **that a man lay down his life for his friends.**"*

Characteristic explained:

Children of God, Believers, are characterized by their commitment and loyalty to the Kingdom of God. **We start and finish tasks.** They don't give up when things are tough or hard. They stick to the task and assignment before them. Loyalty is shown by the extent to which one is prepared to stay committed to someone. **People who are loyal are dependable, faithful and trustworthy. They are defined by their reliability and steadfastness.** Loyal people are constantly steadfast in their dedication.

Life Application:

We all love to have loyal people around us. The best gift we could be to others is to be constantly steadfast in our dedication in our work. We truly value loyalty when we show dependable commitment to stick to a plan even when it proves to be tough to conclude or succeed.

Make a commitment to be someone whom people can depend on, who are faithful and trustworthy. Loyalty is a characteristic of those who truly follow their Lord steadfastly. The question we need to ask ourselves is: *How reliable am I? How trustworthy am I? How steadfast and dependable am I?* Make a decision to be that loyal, reliable and trustworthy friend people can turn to. Be that dependable, faithful and steadfast person.

Prayer:

"Lord, may my loyalty and enduring commitment to You be visible in the way I am dependable, trustworthy and reliable in all that You ask of me. May I be a good representative of this Kingdom Value where I work, and in everything I do."

GRATEFULNESS

Definition:

Gratefulness is the feeling you have, or express, of appreciation for something you have, or received, or observed.

Scriptures:

I Thessalonians 5:18 "**In everything give thanks***: for this is the will of God in Christ Jesus concerning you.*"

Colossians 3:16 (NIV) "16 Let the message of Christ dwell among you richly as you teach and admonish one another with all wisdom through psalms, hymns, and songs from the Spirit, singing to God **with gratitude in your hearts.**"

Psalms 100:4-5 (NIV) 4 **Enter his gates with thanksgiving** *and his courts with praise;* **give thanks to him** *and praise his name. 5 For the Lord is good and his love endures forever; his faithfulness continues through all generations.*

Characteristic explained:

Gratitude is the expression of appreciation and thanks for some blessing one observe in one's life. Gratitude is being thankful. appreciative and grateful. The Psalmist teaches us to enter His Gates with Thanksgiving in our hearts.

Life Application:

We value gratitude when we take time every day and firstly observe the many things we could be grateful for, and secondly, express appreciation to those who made it possible. A question to ask is: *"**Am I a grateful person? How often do I give expression of my gratitude to others and to God, acknowledging them, and Him, for the blessings we observe?**"*

Take time and count your blessings, and if possible give expression to those to whom you are able to express yourself for those blessings. Believers are grateful people. Believers say *"**Thank you.**"* Believers express appreciation and gratitude. Give thanks!

Prayer:

"Lord, I am forever grateful to You for saving me and setting me free. I am forever grateful for Your Love, Your Protection, Your Provision, Your Grace and Mercy in my Life. Thank you for who You are and all the many blessings I share because of You in my life. Thank you for my family, my ministry, my gifts and talents and the opportunities to use them to serve You."

32

STEWARDSHIP

Definition:

Stewardship is proofing oneself faithful as a steward with the Gifts, talents and resources of the King. Stewardship is embracing the accountability, and faithfully administering the resources as directed by the Lord.

Scripture:

Matthew 17:24-27 (NIV) [24] After Jesus and his disciples arrived in Capernaum, the collectors of the two-drachma tax came to Peter and asked, **"Doesn't your teacher pay the temple tax?"** *[25]* **"Yes, he does,"** *he replied. When Peter came into the house, Jesus was the first to speak. "What do you think, Simon?" he asked. "From whom do the kings of the earth collect duty and taxes—from their own sons or from others?" [26] "From others," Peter answered. "Then the* *sons are exempt," Jesus said to him. [27] "But so that we may not offend them, go to the lake and throw out your line. Take the first fish you catch; open its mouth and you will find a four-drachma coin.* **Take it and give it to them for my tax and yours."**

Matthew 22:17-21 (NIV) [17] Tell us then, what is your opinion? **Is it right to pay taxes to Caesar or not?"** *[18] But Jesus, knowing their evil intent, said, "You hypocrites, why are you trying to trap me?[19]* **Show me the coin used for paying the tax.***" They brought him a denarius, [20] and he asked them, "Whose portrait is this? And whose inscription?" [21] "Caesar's," they replied. Then he said to them,* **"Give to Caesar what is Caesar's, and to God what is God's."**

Matthew 25:21 (NIV) "21 "His master replied, **'Well done, good and faithful servant! You have been faithful with a few things; I will put you in charge of many things.** *Come and share your master's happiness!'"*

1 Peter 4:10 (NIV) "10 Each of you should use whatever gift you have received to serve others, **as faithful stewards** *of God's grace in its various forms."*

Characteristic explained:

We value good stewardship when we pay our taxes and honour God with the First fruit of all our income. Stewardship is defined by being a person who have been entrusted with something special, and of worth, and administers the entrustment with faithfulness and care. Stewardship speaks of trustworthiness, reliability and care. Stewardship speaks of noble character.

Life Application:

We are good stewards if we faithfully administer the things God entrusted to us. Joseph was such a faithful steward over the Household of Potiphar. God later rewarded Joseph's faithful Stewardship by entrusting to him the resources of an entire nation. We all have a dream of being welcomed into our eternal home with the words: *"Welcome Home, Good and Faithful Servant."* For us to receive such a welcome we need to see ourselves as stewards, being entrusted with the assets of our Lord. We are not really owners, we are stewards of the entrustments to us. May we be able to show how diligently we administered the gifts, talents and resources he entrusted to us.

A good question to ask, firstly is:

- *What are the things that I believe God entrusted to me?*
- *Am I a good steward of it?*
- *Am I administering it as unto Him and for the advancement of His Kingdom?*

I pray that God will find in each one of us a Faithful and Good Steward.

Prayer

"Father, thank you for entrusting to me the gift of life, good health, a family. Thinking of the things I have beyond food and clothes, with which I am content, I want to thank you for entrusting

me with these. Every good gift comes from You. Thank you for trusting me with so much. I can only pray that I will be a good steward of everything you entrusted to me. Like in the Parable of the Talents, I prayer that I too will use and multiply the talents you have given me. Give me the Wisdom and Favor to Prosper and to have success in bringing increase to what I have in hand. Amen!"

OBEDIENCE

Definition:

*O*bedience is expressed by the way we fully comply and execute that which is expected, asked and demanded of us.

Scripture:

*Luke 11:28 (NIV) "28 He replied, "**Blessed rather are those who hear the word of God and obey it.**"*

*John 8:55 (NIV) "55 Though you do not know him, I know him. If I said I did not, I would be a liar like you, but **I do know him and obey his word.**"*

*John 14:23-24 (NIV) "23 Jesus replied, "**Anyone who loves me will obey my teaching**. My Father will love them, and we will come to them and make our home with them. 24 Anyone who* *does not love me will not obey my teaching. These words you hear are not my own; they belong to the Father who sent me."*

1 Samuel 15:22 (NIV) "**22** So Samuel said: "Has the Lord as great *delight in burnt offerings and sacrifices, As in obeying the voice of the Lord? Behold,* **to obey is better than sacrifice**, *And to heed than the fat of rams."*

Acts 5:29 (NIV) *"29 Peter and the other apostles replied:* "**We must obey God rather than human beings!**"

Acts 5:32 (NIV) *"32 We are witnesses of these things, and so is the Holy Spirit, whom* **God has given to those who obey him.**""

Romans 6:17 (NIV) *"17 But thanks be to God that, though you used to be slaves to sin,* **you have come to obey from your heart the pattern of teaching that has now claimed your allegiance.**"

Matthew 28:20 (NIV) *"20 and* **teaching them to obey everything I have commanded you**. *And surely I am with you always, to the very end of the age.""*

Ephesians 6:1 (NIV) *"1* **Children, obey your parents in the Lord**, *for this is right."*

2 John 1:6 (NIV) *"6 And* **this is love: that we walk in obedience to his commands.** *As you have heard from the beginning, his command is that you walk in love."*

Hebrews 5:8-9 (NIV) "*Son though he was,* **he learned obedience from what he suffered** *9 and, once made perfect,* **he became the source of eternal salvation for all who obey him.**"

Deuteronomy 28:1-13

Characteristic explained:

Obedience is the value of submissive and decisive adherence. Obedience is to respect God by complying and living in agreement with what he said and want. Obedience is the ability to yield and to conform to the Will of Him who Called, Instructed and Directed you to do something. The Blessings of Abraham are reserved for those who walk in obedience to His Will and Purpose.

Life Application:

There is tremendous Power in obedience and submitting to the Will of God. Naaman got healed when he obeyed and went to dip himself in the Jordan River. The widow's debts were paid when she acted in obedience to the Word of the Prophet. Our Salvation was bought by the obedience of our Saviour. We are instructed to teach our Disciples to obey.

Prayer

"*Father, You require obedience more than any sacrifice I make for Your sake, or any offering that I might ever bring to You. I pray that I will obey You from my heart today and every day. May I obey Your Word, the promptings of Your Holy Spirit inside of me, as well as the instructions of those You set in my life to guide and direct me. Give me a willing heart to obey You.*"

CAREFULNESS

Definition:

Carefulness is that considered approach we apply to our words, actions, deeds and thoughts, especially as we consider how it might advance or tarnish the Kingdom of God.

Scripture:

Matthew 16:6 (NIV) "6 "**Be careful**," *Jesus said to them.* "**Be on your guard against the yeast** *of the Pharisees and Sadducees.*"

Colossians 4:5-6 (NIV) "5 **Be wise in the way you act toward outsiders**; *make the most of every opportunity.* 6 **Let your conversation be always full of grace**, *seasoned with salt, so that you may know how to answer everyone.*"

CAREFULNESS | 129

Ephesians 5:15 (NIV) "15 **Be very careful***, then,* **how you live** *—not as unwise but as wise."*

Romans 12:17 (NIV) "17 Do not repay anyone evil for evil. **Be careful to do what is right in the eyes of everyone***."*

1 Corinthians 8:9 (NIV) "9 Be careful, however, that the exercise of your rights does not become a stumbling block to the weak."

Characteristic explained:

Carefulness is the practice of applying care, caution and consideration to one's words, actions, deeds and thoughts, as well as taking care as to what one exposes oneself to.

One the one hand it is an application of *care over how we conduct ourselves* and how our conduct might have a negative bearing on our confession of faith. The care and caution is applied as to not put the Gospel at risk of being slandered as a result of our conduct. On the other hand *watchfulness, alertness and circumspection* is applied as to *what we expose ourselves to*; in particular erroneous teachings, negative and toxic people, and unbecoming relationships.

Carefulness is being Judicious, being prudent in accessing and determining whether we're applying enough care over the welfare and protection of our souls, as well as whether our conduct attests to our faith in Jesus Christ.

Life Application:

1. We value the teaching of Jesus when we apply care as to how we live, and how our conduct helps people, especially weak people, in believing in Him.

2. We value carefulness when we take care of what we listen to, whose teachings and doctrines we expose ourselves

to, and the toxic relational environments we submit ourselves to.

Take care of your conduct daily, and take care as to the influencers you allow into your life. Bad company corrupts good morals.

Prayer

"Father, I come to You in the Wonderful Name of Jesus. I recognize my need of You in every area of my life, especially in keeping me and protecting me under the Shadow of Your Almighty Wings. Give me a wise and discerning heart to apply care and consideration to my thoughts, words and actions as they will affect people around me. May the words of my mouth and the meditation of my heart be acceptable to You. Open my eyes and my understanding to observe areas where I might be vulnerable to the influence of the enemy, and may You give the wisdom, strength and courage to make the mends, take the action and precautions, to be more careful and guarded. I need You Lord Jesus!"

COMPASSION

Definition:

*C*ompassion is the feeling of sorrow or pity for **someone,** and expressed by showing them kindness, mercy, sympathy or tenderness.

Scripture:

Matthew 9:36 (NIV) "36 When he saw the crowds, **he had compassion on them,** *because they were harassed and helpless, like sheep without a shepherd."*

1 Peter 3:8 "Finally, be ye all of one mind, **having compassion one of another,** *love as brethren, be pitiful, be courteous:"*

Exodus 33:19 (NIV) "19 And the Lord said, "I will cause all my goodness to pass in front of you, and I will proclaim my name, the Lord, in your presence. I will have mercy on whom I will have mercy, and **I will have compassion on whom I will have compassion.**"

Psalms 116:5 (NIV) "5 The Lord is gracious and righteous; **our God is full of compassion.**"

Exodus 22:26-27 (NIV) "26 If you take your neighbour's` cloak as a pledge, return it by sunset, 27 because that cloak is the only covering your neighbor has. What else can they sleep in? When they cry out to me, I will hear, **for I am compassionate.**"

Psalms 86:15 (NIV) "15 But you, **Lord, are a compassionate and gracious God**, *slow to anger, abounding in love and faithfulness."*

Colossians 3:12 (NIV) "12 Therefore, as God's chosen people, holy and dearly loved, **clothe yourselves with compassion**, *kindness, humility, gentleness and patience."*

Philippians 2:1-2 (NIV) "1 Therefore if you have any encouragement from being united with Christ, if any comfort from his love, if any common sharing in the Spirit, if any tenderness and **compassion,** *2 then* **make my joy complete by being like-minded, having the same love, being one in spirit and of one mind.**"

Characteristic explained:

WHAT WE LEARNT about the Nature and Character of God from the beginning was His great Compassion for His people. On numerous occasions we see His love and Compassion expressed towards His people. Compassion is the show of sympathy, concern and empathy towards others in their distress or shortcomings.

To be Compassionate is to be kind-hearted and concerned with care for those around us. Compassion is showing consideration for the needs and care of others. We can see this compassionate care in the life of Christ expressed towards people on a number of occasions. He expressed it when He observed that they were like sheep without a Shepherd. He had compassion on the people when they were with Him for a few days without eating. He was concerned for their welfare. In the Apostle Paul's address to the Church in Philippi he exhorted them, through their union with Christ, to be "like-minded" and "have the same love" that they were comforted with through their union with Christ.

Life Application:

We value our relationship and union with Christ by walking in His footsteps, and desiring to life and be like Him. One of the ways in which we give credence to this union with Christ is by being compassionate. Take time to show kind-heartedness and care towards people around you on a daily basis. Take time to look for the challenges people face around you. May the challenges people face move us with the same compassion Christ is moved to help us in our weaknesses. Show concern, sympathy and understanding for the weaknesses people face daily. One of the most powerful ways in which we can show our true compassion, like Christ, is to help people in their weaknesses. See how you can help and assist people wherever you find yourself. Helping and giving a willing listening ear to listen to cries of people is sometimes the biggest show of compassion and care they need and require. Take time to care and be kind.

Prayer

"Father, I come to You in the Name of the Lord Jesus. Father, I want to be like You and the Lord Jesus. I ask You to fill me with Your Compassion and considered care. may I be gracious and compassionate in my dealings with those who fall and fail around me. May I be an instrument in Your hands to show compassion to people who need to experience Your love and care around me. May I show concern, sympathy and understanding for those who are weak and in need today. May I be filled with Your Compassion and Care? Amen"

CARING

Definition:

Caring is being thoughtful, sympathetic and lovingly helpful towards others, especially considering their cares, burdens and concerns.

Scripture:

Galatians 6:2 (NIV) "2 **Carry each other's burdens**, *and in this way you will fulfill the law of Christ."*

1 Peter 5:2-3 (NIV) 2 **Be shepherds of God's flock** *that is under your care, watching over them—not because you must, but because you are willing, as God wants you to be; not pursuing dishonest gain, but eager to serve; 3 not lording it over those entrusted to you, but being examples to the flock."*

> *1 Timothy 5:4 (NIV) "4 But if a widow has children or grandchildren, these should learn first of all to* **put their religion into practice by caring for their own family** *and so repaying their parents and grandparents, for this is pleasing to God."*

> *John 21:16 (NIV) "16 Again Jesus said, "Simon son of John, do you love me?" He answered, "Yes, Lord, you know that I love you." Jesus said,* **"Take care of my sheep**.*"""*

Characteristic explained:

Being caring is being mindful, considerate and helpful to others. Being Caring is to be lovingly concerned for the welfare of others. To be caring is to be sensitive to the needs and cares of others, and to treat them with compassion. One of the characteristics Jesus desired His Disciples to have was to "take care" of His sheep. To put it into the Words of Paul to Timothy, to "take care" is to put our religion into practice. We do what we value. Well, one of those true values in the Kingdom of God is to take care of those around you, and under your care.

Life Application:

We show care firstly when we take note of the cares, concerns and burdens people around us, especially those entrusted to our care, have. Secondly, we take care when we do something about it, by showing love, being helpful and assisting.

To be caring is to be mindful and considerate in a way that shows those concerned that you really care. We take care when we carry each other's burdens. One of the ways is to relief the burden from a working single parent by offering to look after their children to enable them to go and work, enabling them to earn a wage without having to add more pressure of having to pay for childcare.

ANOTHER WAY IS to assist with providing temporary care for people with aging parents. Every time we step up to meet the needs of others, especially when we've taken the time to notice their distress and need of help, we honour God by providing care. Take care of each other, and carry each other's burdens, and in this way fulfill the way of love.

Prayer

"Father, You are a Caring Father. I thank You for Your Care over me and my family. May I carry the same Care, consideration and understanding into every situation I face today. May people around me know that You care for them by the way I represent You in my dealings with people. May I care in a tangible way wherever i go today!"

CONFIDENT

Definition:

Confidence is the trust and faith you have in someone or something. It is a strong belief and feeling of certainty with which you do things.

Scripture:

*Philippians 1:6 (NIV) "6 **being confident of this, that he who began a good work in you will carry it on to completion until the day of Christ Jesus.**"*

*2 Corinthians 3:4 (NIV) "4 **Such confidence we have through Christ** before God."*

*Ephesians 3:12 (NIV) "12 In him and through faith in him we may approach God with freedom and **confidence.**"*

Hebrews 4:16 (NIV) "16 Let us then **approach God's throne of grace with confidence**, *so that we may receive mercy and find grace to help us in our time of need.*"

Hebrews 3:14 (NIV) "*14 We have come to share in Christ,* **if indeed we hold our original conviction firmly** *to the very end.*"

Hebrews 3:6 (NIV) "*6 But Christ is faithful as the Son over God's house. And we are his house, if indeed* **we hold firmly to our confidence and the hope** *in which we glory.*"

Hebrews 10:19 (NIV) "*19 Therefore, brothers and sisters, since* **we have confidence to enter the Most Holy Place by the blood of Jesus,**"

Hebrews 10:35 (NIV) "35 **So do not throw away your confidence;** *it will be richly rewarded.*"

Hebrews 11:1 (NIV) Faith in Action "*1 Now* **faith is confidence** *in what we hope for and assurance about what we do not see.*"

Philippians 1:6 (NIV) "*6* **being confident of this,** *that he who began a good work in you will carry it on to completion until the day of Christ Jesus.*"

Characteristic explained:

God is the source of confidence, and as we place our indisputable trust and faith in Him, He works this confidence in us to do extra-ordinary things. Hebrews 11 verse one starts by saying: *"Now faith is confidence…"* Confidence is to have faith in someone or something. ***Confidence is that assurance*** of how sure you are, to *the extent that you will act on the confidence you have*, especially as it relates to our faith and confidence in what God said in His Word, and therefor we act upon His Word. *Confidence is expressed by the certainty with which you act* and do things. Confidence is that self-reliant, self-confident act in assurance of faith. In other words *you do because you are convinced* **and** *assured.*

Life Application:

Faith is confidence in what we hope for to be true. We give expression to our faith by the confident way upon which we act upon the Words and Instructions of the Bible. There is a direct correlation between the faith we have and the confidence with which we carry ourselves. Never loose your confidence in the things you've become assured of, especially about your faith in God and His Word. Act in confidence. *May our confidence show others how strong your faith in God really is.*

Prayer

"Father, I have confidence in coming to You today because of the Blood of Jesus. I have confidence because You allow me to come before You in Your Holy Presence every day. Thank you for this privilege and honour. Father, confidence comes from You. I pray that You will make me and fill me with Your confidence and strength to be a consistent Witness for You. I pray for Your Confidence today."

STEADFASTNESS

Definition:

Steadfastness is the inner assertiveness to be firmly fixed and focused on doing what you purposed to do. It is the ability to be constant and unchanging in your course of faith and action.

Scripture:

Matthew 10:22 (NIV) "22 You will be hated by everyone because of me, but **the one who stands firm to the end will be saved.**"

Matthew 24:12-13 (NIV) "12 Because of the increase of wickedness, the love of most will grow cold, 13 but **the one who stands firm to the end will be saved.**"

Hebrews 10:23 (NIV) "23 **Let us hold unswervingly to the hope we profess,** *for he who promised is faithful."*

1 Corinthians 15:58 (NIV) "58 *Therefore, my dear brothers and sisters,* **stand firm. Let nothing move you. Always give yourselves fully to the work of the Lord,** *because you know that your labour in the Lord is not in vain.*

2 Thessalonians 2:15 (NIV) "15 *So then, brothers and sisters,* **stand firm and hold fast to the teachings we passed on to you,** *whether by word of mouth or by letter."*

Isaiah 26:3 (NIV) "3 *You will keep in perfect peace* **those whose minds are steadfast,** *because they trust in you."*

Characteristic explained:

Steadfastness is that loyal and firm commitment to keep firmly to your beliefs. Steadfastness is to be uncompromisingly firm in one's convictions. Steadfastness is that persistent, loyal resoluteness to stay the course. Firmness speaks of consistency and dependability. Firmness is expressed in us being inflexible, uncompromising rigid, and determined to hold on to what we belief, and the principles we determined to live our lives by.

Life Application:

How do we give expression to this Kingdom value?
Firstly, by subscribing and determining to learn, adopt and live by the values and principles of the Bible.
Secondly, we give expression to Firmness or Steadfastness

by intentionally putting the principles and values, of the Biblically learnt values, before our preferences, habitual reactions or responses.

Thirdly, by developing a resoluteness, because of how it pleases God when we stand by the values of the Kingdom of God, to maintain and be loyal to your decision to do things according to what the Bible teaches. God desires us to be predetermined and resolute in our following of Him.

As much as what the world nowadays cries foul over Christians being so inconsiderate and unkind to block legislature to adopt abnormal behavior and practices, as normal and acceptable, I pray that we will all stand firm on the teachings of Christ. Don't let the assaults weaken you in your resoluteness to keep to the Principles of the Bible. I wish to conclude this short deliberation with one of the first teachings of our Lord when He was teaching His Disciples on the Mountain:

> *Matthew 5:10-12 (NIV)* [10] **Blessed are those who are persecuted because of righteousness,** *for theirs is the kingdom of heaven.* [11] **"Blessed are you when people insult you, persecute you and falsely say all kinds of evil against you because of me.** [12] *Rejoice and be glad, because* **great is your reward in heaven,** *for in the same way they persecuted the prophets who were before you.*

Prayer

"Father, I pray that I will be one of those who stand uncompromisingly firm in my decisions to follow the teachings of Your Son, Jesus. I pray that I will stand firm in my faith in You. I pray that I will be steadfast in fulfilling what You called me to do. May I stand strong in my faith, unwavering, despite the persecutions, insults or false accusations I might face. May I be known as a Steadfast Believer."

CONTENTMENT

Definition:

Contentment is the pre-positioning and determination of being satisfied and pleased regardless of the circumstances you might find yourself in. Contentment is the satisfaction with one's current state.

Scripture:

Matthew 6:25 (NIV) "25 "Therefore I tell you, **do not worry about your life, what you will eat or drink; or about your body, what you will wear**. *Is not life more than food, and the body more than clothes?*

1 Timothy 6:6 (NIV) "6 But **godliness with contentment is great gain**."

1 Timothy 6:8 (NIV) "8 But ***if we have food and* clothing, we will be content with that.**"

Philippians 4:11-12 (NIV) "11 I am not saying this because I am in need, for **I have learned to be content whatever the circumstances.** *12 I know what it is to be in need, and I know what it is to have plenty.* **I have learned the secret of being content in any and every situation,** *whether well fed or hungry, whether living in plenty or in want."*

Characteristic explained:

Contentment is a learnt value, like every other Value. *To be content is to be satisfied with what you have.* It is a pre-determination that if you have food, something to drink, and clothes to wear, that you have everything you need to live, and with that in mind, to be grateful for everything else beyond that.

Life Application:

How content am I? People love to be around people who are content with what they have. There is a balance to strike between being content with what you have and what you don't have. Many people live so focused on what they don't have that they always present themselves, not willingly, as deprived people. I love to be around people who are satisfied with what they have. This does not mean that they don't aspire for more, or for bigger and better things, no, their satisfaction and contentment outweighs the bearing of their wants and desires. May we live content with what we have, with that which our Father in Heaven blessed us with.

Prayer

"Father, I come before You with a Grateful heart today. I am grateful that I have more than what I need or deserve. Teach me to

be content with what I have and not to allow the want for the things I desire and don't have to outweigh my gratitude and contentment. Teach me to be content with what I have and what You've given me."

TEACHABLE

Definition:

To be Teachable is to be willing to learn and change and be transformed in condition, character, form or appearance, especially into the likeness of Christ.

Scripture:

Matthew 11:29 (NIV) *²⁹ Take my yoke upon you and* **learn from me**, *for I am gentle and humble in heart, and you will find rest for your souls.*

John 6:45 (NIV) *⁴⁵ It is written in the Prophets:* **'They will all be taught by God.'** *Everyone who has heard the Father and learned from him comes to me."*

Colossians 3:10 (NIV) *"10 and have* **put on the new self,** *which* **is being renewed in knowledge in the image of its Creator."**

> *John 14:26 (NIV) "**26** But the Helper, **the Holy Spirit**, whom the Father will send in My name, **He will teach you all things**, and bring to your remembrance all things that I said to you."*
>
> *Romans 12:2 "And be not conformed to this world: but **be ye transformed by the renewing of your mind**, that ye may prove what is that good, and acceptable, and perfect, will of God."*
>
> *Ephesians 4:22-24 (NIV) "22 You were taught, with regard to your former way of life, to put off your old self, which is being corrupted by its deceitful desires; 23 to be made new in the attitude of your minds; 24 and to **put on the new self**, created to be like God in true righteousness and holiness."*

Characteristic explained:

We are Teachable when we open our hearts to be renewed in our minds. Only a commitment to being renewed in the spirit of your mind will ensure a lifetime of being teachable. Transformation takes place when we determinately put off our old self, and determinately put on the new self.

We become what we pursue in our minds and in our hearts. For us as Believers it is the determination to get rid of the old worldly nature and to constantly open ourselves to be renewed our minds with the things of God.

In each of these instances where we read about the process of Transformation, it is really a matter of putting the things that was taught into practice, and that requires us to remain Teachable. The more we willingly put things into the forefront of our minds, the more we change and transform.

Life Application:

I LOVE the way the writer to the Romans puts it; *"Be ye transformed"*. To be Teachable is about a constant decision to change, and a determination to not conform to the pattern of this world. To be teachable requires us to transform. Conforming is the result of accepting the ways of the world as the norm and you simply complying, however, on the other hand, transformation happens when we are teachable and actively engage in embracing the values of the Kingdom of God as our own, and putting them into practice.

Ask yourself the question, in every decision that confronts your moral standing, whether you are conforming or transforming.

- *Am I conforming or being transformed?*

I saw this characteristic in one of my Pastor's, their ability to adopt new ways of doing things, and adapting to changing circumstances as well as flowing with the way the Spirit works within the Church. One simple example was with the way in which he responded to the operation of the gifts of the Holy Spirit within his churches.

The question remains:

- *How Teachable am I?*
- *How open am I to receive correction or instruction?*

Prayer

"Heavenly Father, I come to You in the Wonderful Name of the Lord Jesus. I have learned so much from Your example Jesus. I pray that I will always be flexible and will continue to be transformed by Your Word and Your Holy Spirit's work in my life. May I continue to be Teachable today. May my heart be open to learn and be open to

move with what You want to do in my life. Teach me Lord, I want to learn from You, through Your Word and from Your Holy Spirit."

DEFERENCE

Definition:

*D*eference is the considered and thoughtful action of living an exemplary life with the expressed purpose of leading others to Christ through your way of living in constant reference to Him and His Word.

Scripture:

Matthew 5:16 (NIV) "16 In the same way, **let your light shine before others, that they may see your good deeds and glorify your Father in heaven.**"

John 5:30 (NIV) "30 By myself I can do nothing; I judge only as I hear, and my judgment is just, for **I seek not to please myself but him who sent me.**"

> *James 4:15 (NIV) "15 Instead, you ought to say, "***If it is the Lord's will, we will live and do this or tha***t."*
>
> *1 Corinthians 9:22 (NIV) "22 To the weak I became weak, to win the weak. I have become all things to all people so* **that by all possible means I might save some.***"*
>
> *I Corinthians 10:33 "Even as I please all men in all things,* ***not seeking mine own profit, but the profit of many, that they may be saved."***
>
> *Romans 14:13 (NIV) "13 Therefore let us stop passing judgment on one another. Instead,* **make up your mind not to put any stumbling block or obstacle in the way of a brother or sister."**
>
> *Ephesians 5:1-2 (NIV) 1* **Follow God's example***, therefore, as dearly loved children 2 and* ***walk in the way of love, just as Christ loved us and gave himself up for us*** *as a fragrant offering and sacrifice to God.*

Characteristic explained:

Deference is the expression of awe and adoration for someone or something, with the expressed purpose of leading others into the same allegiance. Deference refers to the intentional way we show others who we have a high regard for. Deference is the showing of esteemed respect and regard for a person and His teachings or views.

Deference living is the expressed value of living in strong reference to the Bible, and is expressed by one's submission to it. Our lives should strongly reflect our allegiance to the Bible and especially the teachings of Jesus. Deference living is living a life that point people to Christ, and shows others that we live in submission to Him and His Word. Jesus modeled this to us throughout His earthly ministry. When tempted by the Devil, He referred to the Scriptures. When questioned about His Authority, He pointed to the One who sent Him and whose instructions and Will He fulfills.

Deference means to show submission, allegiance and compliance, but also reverence, awe and regard. For us as Believers it is the constant using of every opportunity to point people to the One we adore and value as the Supreme Leader and Authority in our lives, like Jesus did.

Life Application:

A value is only valued if practiced and observed in one's daily life.

A good question to ask and answer to yourself today is:

- *How am I, through my words and deeds show others that I greatly value and honour God and His Word in my life?*
- *How can I give expression to this Deference more?*

We do what we value. Our values are seen and observed by what we say and do. Every time we refer to the Bible as our point of reference for guidance, we practice deference. Every time we say: *"If the Lord willing,"* we practice deference, and give expression to our high regard for living in Favour with Him. Every time we give honour to the Lord when things turn out for good, or when something good happens, we practice deference.

Deference is the active giving of honour, and expressing gratitude to the Lord in every situation that shows others that we truly value God, His Son, the Holy Spirit and the Word, in our lives.

Now, let's think again on ways in which we can actively bring honour to God through our words and deeds today.

Prayer

"Father God, My prayer is that people will quickly know, through my actions, words and conversations that I belong to You and that I hold You in the highest place and regard in my life. May my deference to You and Your Word point people to You. I love You more than anything and everyone. You mean the world to me and I want everyone to know that. Amen!"

DILIGENCE

Definition:

*D*iligence is the paying of careful and unceasing attention to doing things well. Diligence is developed in us by paying attention and being conscientious in everything we do.

Scripture:

John 4:34 (NIV) "34 "My food," said Jesus, "is **to do the will of him who sent me** *and* **to finish his work**."

Colossians 3:23 "And **whatsoever ye do, do it heartily, as to the Lord**, *and not unto men.*

1 Thessalonians 4:11-12 (NIV) 11 and to **make it your ambition to lead a quiet life**: *You should mind your own business and work with your hands, just as we told you, 12* **so that your**

daily life may win the respect of outsiders *and so that you will not be dependent on anybody.*

Ecclesiastes 9:10 (NIV) "10 **Whatever your hand finds to do, do it with all your might,** *for in the realm of the dead, where you are going, there is neither working nor planning nor knowledge nor wisdom."*

Colossians 3:22-24 (NIV) "22 Slaves, obey your earthly masters in everything; and do it, not only when their eye is on you and to curry their favor, **but with sincerity of heart and reverence for the Lord.** *23 Whatever you do,* **work at it with all your heart, as working for the Lord**, *not for human masters, 24 since you know that you will receive an inheritance from the Lord as a reward.* **It is the Lord Christ you are serving.***"*

Characteristic explained:

Diligence is the practice of careful and attentive thoroughness. To be diligent is to be persistently meticulous. It is to be tirelessly working at things until it is done. Jesus was diligent in finishing the tasks set before Him. He modeled working tirelessly and diligently to seek and save the lost and to finish the course of His Life with excellence. He was diligent to the end. God desires that we apply this same endurance of diligence to our work ethics. We need to finish what we start. We are diligent not only in completing tasks, but in completing them with the right attitude as well. Diligent people always do that extra bit. You are diligent when you apply yourself to every task wholeheartedly, and with such devotion that it attracts the respect of outsiders.

Life Application:

We all have tasks to do today. These might be formal required tasks, like doing your job for which you are paid, or informal casually required tasks like doing the dishes or laundry. The thing to consider is whether I am giving credence to this value in my approach to the tasks at hand. Diligence requires the right attitude in that I do everything as unto the Lord. Diligence also requires me to do things to the best of my abilities, not half-hearted or just to get it over and done. Diligence requires a constant focus on who I am doing things for. It requires sincerity of heart and reverence for the Lord. Let us earnestly consider the diligence we apply to the tasks before us today, and every day, regardless of who we perform them for.

Prayer

"Father God, I pray that You will find in me a diligent Servant of Yours, always doing thing from my heart in devotion to You. May the way in which I work and do things reflect my devotion to You. May I be diligent in finishing tasks that You gave me to do."

TRUSTWORTHINESS

Definition:

*T*rustworthiness is truthfulness and faithfulness combined. This is a rewarded characteristic of Believers. Believers are known for their trustworthiness, truthfulness and faithfulness.

Scripture:

Matthew 25:21 (NIV) "21 "His master replied, **'Well done, good and faithful servant! You have been faithful with a few things**; *I will put you in charge of many things. Come and share your master's happiness!'*

1 Timothy 6:20 (NIV) "20 **Timothy, guard what has been entrusted to your care**. *Turn away from godless chatter and the opposing ideas of what is falsely called knowledge,*"

1 Corinthians 4:2 (NIV) **"2** *Now* **it is required that those who have been given a trust must prove faithful.**"

Characteristic explained:

Trustworthiness is the practice of good stewardship over the gifts, talents and resources we have. Trustworthiness is the practice of honesty and reliability. Trustworthiness is defined by being constantly dependably and responsible. Credibility is one of the key characteristics of someone who is trustworthy.

The extent to which we take responsibility is seen in the way we treat the feelings and possessions of others. Most people take care of their own things, but not everyone is as attentive to take care of the possessions of another. In the Kingdom of God we embrace the fact that everything belongs to God, and that we are purely entrusted stewards of what belongs to Him. For Believers, it is essential that we practice the taking of responsibility and that we live to be worthy of more trust.

Life Application:

The question therefor to ask oneself is:

- *Am I a constantly reliable person upon whom others can depend?*
- *Am I honest and credible?*
- *Do I take responsibility for things I do and are involved in?*

It should be our desire and intention to be people whom God can trust with His most treasured Gifts. Take responsibility for your actions, reactions and words today. Live, and conduct yourself in such a way that it will show people that you are worthy of their trust. They can depend on you since you are constantly reliable and dependable.

Prayer

"Father God, You know me. You know know all my thoughts and the words of my mouth before they are formed on my tongue. My prayer is that I will walk before You in truth and faithfulness so that I could be found trustworthy in every area of my life. Truthfulness and Faithfulness is instilled by Your Holy Spirit on the inside of our hearts. May You, by Your Holy Spirit give me a Spirit of Truthfulness and Faithfulness that I might be found Trustworthy every day? I want You to find in me a Faithful Servant worthy of Your Trust. Amen"

GENTLENESS

Definition:

Gentleness is the ability to be patient and kind, and expressed by a continual compassionate leniency towards all people.

Scripture:

Matthew 11:29 (NIV) "29 Take my yoke upon you and **learn from me**, *for* **I am gentle and humble in heart**, *and you will find rest for your souls."*

2 Timothy 2:24 "And the servant of the Lord must not strive; but **be gentle** *unto all men, apt to teach, and patient."*

Galatians 5:22-23 (NIV) "22 But the fruit of the Spirit is love, joy, peace, **forbearance***, kindness, goodness, faithfulness, 23* **gentleness** *and self-control. Against such things there is no law."*

Philippians 4:5 (NIV) "5 **Let your gentleness be evident to all***. The Lord is near."*

Colossians 3:12-14 (NIV) "12 Therefore, as God's chosen people, holy and dearly loved, **clothe yourselves with** *compassion, kindness, humility,* **gentleness** *and patience. 13 Bear with each other and forgive one another if any of you has a grievance against someone. Forgive as the Lord forgave you. 14 And* **over all these virtues** *put on love, which binds them all together in perfect unity."*

1 Timothy 6:11 (NIV) "11 **But you, man of God***, flee from all this, and* **pursue** *righteousness, godliness, faith, love, endurance and* **gentleness***."*

Characteristic explained:

G<small>ENTLENESS IS</small> **the practice of tenderness.** Gentleness is practiced when we are calm and approach situations with kindness. Having a softer approach is prized as gentleness. God desires us to be gentle in our dealings with people, but also to be gentle in how we handle difficult and complex situations. One of the greatest expressions and examples of this was the way in which Jesus handled the woman who was caught in adultery. He had a gentler approach with her. Being gentle is to practice forbearance, to be gracious and determinately soft.

Life Application:

God desires that those who profess Him as Lord, in in whom He deposited His Holy Spirit will be gentle, and that their gentleness be seen and know to all.
The question to answer to yourself is:

- *"Do I allow the gentleness of Christ to be made known to others around me?"*
- *"Am I intentionally, and thoughtfully gentle in difficult situations?"*
- *"How can I let my gentleness be more visible to others, as Christ want me to be?"*
- *"What does the gentleness of Christ looks like, and am I learning from Him on how to be gentle and kind?"*

The thoughtful and considered answering to these questions in my life will most certainly leave me gentler in nature and conduct.

Prayer

"Father God, I come to you in the Name of the Lord Jesus. Father, I want to learn from You and Your Word today on how to be gentle. Your Word says that I should "clothe myself with gentleness", I pray for Your help in reminding me to be gentle in my conversations, my thoughts, my actions, my attitudes, and all my dealings with people today. I pray for much forbearance and a soft approach with those who fall and fail around me. may I be Gentle like You are with me when I fail You and Fall. May I show Your Gentleness in every conversation, every response and every action or reaction of mine today. Fill me and teach me how to be Gentle like You are. Amen!"

DISCERNMENT

Definition:

*D*iscernment is the ability to distinguish between right and wrong, between what is more expedient or not, and what is best. Discernment is also the ability to see the difference between things and to understand clearly the distinction between thoughts, ideas and concepts.

Scripture:

Philippians 1:10 (NIV) "10 **so that you may be able to discern what is best and may be pure and blameless** *for the day of Christ,"*

Philippians 1:9-11 (NIV) "9 And **this is my prayer**: *that your love may abound more and more in knowledge and depth of insight,* 10 **so that you may be able to discern what is best and may be pure and blameless** *for the* *day of Christ, 11* **filled with the fruit of righteousness** *that comes through Jesus Christ —to the glory and praise of God."*

Hebrews 5:14 (NIV) "14 But solid food is for the mature, **who by constant use have trained themselves to distinguish good from evil."**

Ezekiel 44:23 (NIV) "23 **They are to teach my people the difference between the holy and the common and show them how to distinguish between the unclean and the clean."**

Psalms 119:125 (NIV) "125 I am your servant; **give me discernment that I may understand your statutes***."*

1 Corinthians 12:10 (NIV) "10 to another miraculous powers, to another prophecy, **to another distinguishing between spirits,** *to another speaking in different kinds of tongues, and to still another the interpretation of tongues."*

Characteristic explained:

Discernment is the ability to make sensitive decisions based on sound and selective judgement. Discernment is the applied ability to judge for yourself between things. The Bible teaches that this is both an applied and developing value, as well as a gift God gives us, especially in regards to spiritual things. Our constant application of this value will help us greatly to make wise and enduring decisions.

Discernment is the ability to distinguish between what is

good and what is evil and to value making a choice for the good. Discernment deals particularly with making good, positive and up building choices. People who don't apply discernment to their lives live carelessly and are often surprised when the impact of their careless and thoughtless actions and words become known.

Life Application:

We all face the making of decisions between good and evil every day. Applying this value is to recognize whether we are deciding for good rather than for evil. Hebrews 5 tells us that it is an acquired value by practicing to choose good over evil. We mature in our faith when we apply this skill diligently.

It is beneficial to ask oneself:

- **Is it helpful?**
- **Is it going to impact people positively?**
- **Will people be built up through this decision?**
- **Will it be beneficial?**
- **Is this a positive decision?**

Anything other than a positive and affirmative answer to any of these probing questions will leave you erring in applying discernment. Mature people apply great discernment to their lives. Their ability to discern makes them people with understanding.

Prayer:

"Father, I come to You today in the Name of Jesus. Father, I pray that You will give me a wise and discerning heart. I pray for discernment with the decisions that I face today. Help me to make decisions in accordance with Your will. May Your Holy Spirit guide me to make decisions for the good and upbuilding of others. Help me to understand and to discern the spiritual atmosphere wherever I

go, that I will be prepared in spirit and in my mind to deal with varied spiritual atmospheres daily. Help me to see those areas where I might be blinded by the deceitfulness of the enemy. Help me to discern the hearts of those with whom I daily meet. I need so much discernment in the day that I am living in as to know the heart of those I work with and minister to. I need You Lord!"

TRUTHFULNESS

Definition:

Truthfulness is the ability to speak and act in an honest, open, just, reliable and righteous way.

Scripture:

Matthew 22:16 (NIV) "16 They sent their disciples to him along with the Herodians. "Teacher," they said, **"we know that you are a man of integrity and that you teach the way of God in accordance with the truth.** *You aren't swayed by others, because you pay no attention to who they are."*

Ephesians 4:25 "Wherefore putting away lying, **speak every man truth with his neighbour:** *for we are members one of another."*

Psalms 15:2 (NIV) "2 The one whose walk is blameless, who does what is righteous, **who speaks the truth from their heart;**"

Proverbs 22:20-21 (NIV) "20 Have I not written thirty sayings for you, sayings of counsel and knowledge, 21 **teaching you to be honest** *and* **to speak the truth***, so that you bring back truthful reports to those you serve?"*

1 Corinthians 4:17 (NIV) "17 For this reason I have sent to you Timothy, my son whom I love, who is faithful in the Lord. **He will remind you of my way of life in Christ Jesus, which agrees with what I teach everywhere in every church.**"

Characteristic explained:

To be truthful is to be honest, straight, open, true and reliable. To be truthful is to speak reliable facts as they are. Truthfulness is one of the key essential values of someone who hold high integrity and character. Truthful people speak ingeniously open and straight. They say things as they are and not as people want to hear them, neither do they add their own slant to it. Truthfulness also relates to one's actions, that they are consistent with the faith and integrity you profess. Truthful people live with integrity to their moral standing and faith.

Life Application:

We are truthful when we speak what is true and reliable. We are truthful when we are honest and open. We are truthful when we uphold facts with integrity of conscience. May we always tell things in a way that is reliable and true to the facts. Truthfulness should be reflected in the way we live before all people, and in all circumstances. Truthful people live the same, and speak the same at church as what they live and speak at home.

Whenever we say something we should ask ourselves whether it is the truth, consistent with the facts? We should consider our actions and behaviour before all men, as to whether they truly reflect who we are and what we stand for. Live in such a way that you can maintain your peace at all times.

Prayer:

"Father God, I thank You that You are the Truth, the Life, and the Way! I honor You today as the source and example of living, modeling and speaking the Truth. I pray that I will uphold Your Truth in every area of my Life. Your Word is the Truth. I declare that my experiences sometimes does not override Your truth, and I submit myself to learn more to know Your Truth. I also pray that I will live truthfully and consistently with the faith I placed in You. May I speak the truth in every situation today. May I live to be known as a truthful and honest person, even when it sometimes make me feel embarrassed and ashamed. May I uphold Your Truth in my words, my actions and my deeds. May I speak the Truth from my heart, live truthfully and honor You as the observer of every conversation. Amen!"

GENEROSITY

Definition:

Generosity is the ability to be unselfish with a readiness to share and to give freely.

Scripture:

Matthew 10:8 (NIV) "8 Heal the sick, raise the dead, cleanse those who have leprosy, drive out demons. **Freely you have received; freely give.**"

Matthew 25:34-36 (NIV) "34 "Then the King will say to those on his right, 'Come, you who are blessed by my Father; take your inheritance, the kingdom prepared for you since the creation of the world. 35 For **I was hungry** *and* **you gave me something to eat, I was thirsty** *and* **you gave me something to drink, I was a stranger** *and* **you invited me in,** *36 I needed* clothes *and* you clothed me, I was sick *and* you looked after me, I was in prison *and* you came to visit me.'"

Acts 20:35 (NIV) "35 In everything I did, I showed you that by this kind of hard work we must help the weak, **remembering the words the Lord Jesus himself** *said:* **'It is more blessed to give than to receive."**

Acts 2:44-45 (NIV) "⁴⁴ **All the believers** *were together and* **had everything in common.** *⁴⁵* **They sold property and possessions to give to anyone who had need.**"

Acts 4:32-35 (NIV) "³² All the believers were one in heart and mind. **No one claimed that any of their possessions was their own, but they shared everything they had.** *³³ With great power the apostles continued to testify to the resurrection of the Lord Jesus. And God's grace was so powerfully at work in them all ³⁴ that there were no needy persons among them.* **For from time to time those who owned land or houses sold them, brought the money from the sales ³⁵ and put it at the apostles' feet**, *and it was distributed to anyone who had need."*

2 Corinthians 8:2-4, 6 (NIV) "2 In the midst of a very severe trial, their overflowing joy and **their extreme poverty welled up in rich generosity.** *3 For I testify that* **they gave as much as they were able, and even beyond their ability.** *Entirely on their own, 4 they* *urgently pleaded with us for the privilege of sharing in this service to the Lord's people. 6 Remember this: Whoever sows sparingly will also reap sparingly, and* **whoever sows generously will also reap generously."**

2 Corinthians 9:11 (NIV) "11 You will be enriched in every way so that **you can be generous on every occasion,** *and* **through us your generosity will result in thanksgiving to God."**

2 Corinthians 9:13 (NIV) "13 **Because of the service by which you have proved yourselves,** *others will praise God for the obedience that accompanies your confession of the gospel of Christ,* **and for your generosity in sharing with them and with everyone else."**

Characteristic explained:

Generosity is a way of expressing gratitude for the gifts and blessings we share in life, by giving back. Generosity is the act of kindness by being open-handed and liberal in our giving of kindness. Generosity is expressed when we give cheerfully. Generosity is expressed in everything we do, whether that be in being gracious, compassionate, loving or faithful, in fact, whatever we do, let us be generous in the expression of our giving.

Generosity is the expression of a heart attitude. Some people think that you have to be wealthy to be generous, but I have seen more generosity among poor people than among the wealthy. The example of the Macedonians shows us the true heart of the generous spirit that they gave with joy, in spite of extreme poverty. The early church practiced this generosity in the way they shared, and had everything in common.

Life Application:

When we give ourselves, and of ourselves liberally then we are generous. *Every time we show kindness unreservedly, we are generous.* Generosity is the opening of our heart to show and express kindness. Generosity is shown when we heartily apply ourselves in every situation to see what we can do, and do it.

Generous people give unreservedly! Generous people are Sowers, they value the seed they have, and they sow it. Search your heart and look for ways in which you could show generosity.

Prayer:

"Father God, You are the most Generous person I know. Your Generosity knows no boundaries. Out of my gratefulness for Your daily showing of how generous You are, may I be and instrument in Your Hands to show generosity to those around me today. May I be generous in showing Your love, may I be generous in being Gracious and compassionate and in kindness. May I be generous in being forbearing and forgiving. May I be generous in using the gifts and talents You've given to to build and encourage others today. May I also continue to be generous with the seed you've placed in my hands to bless others. May I be known as a generous person."

KINDNESS

Definition:

Kindness is that generally warm-hearted, friendly and well-meaning interaction with others. Kindness is seen in the thoughtfulness and consideration with which we deal with people.

Scripture:

Ephesians 4:32 (NIV) "32 **Be kind and compassionate to one another**, *forgiving each other, just as in Christ God forgave you.*"

Colossians 3:12 (NIV) "12 Therefore, as God's chosen people, holy and dearly loved, clothe yourselves with compassion, **kindness**, humility, gentleness and patience."

*Galatians 5:22 (NIV) "22 But the fruit of the Spirit is love, joy, peace, forbearance, **kindness**, goodness, faithfulness,"*

Characteristic explained:

The key characteristics of those who embrace kindness is that they are considerate, caring, kind-hearted, and sympathetic in the way they deal with others. Kindness is expressed by being gentle, thoughtful and humane in dealing with people.

Life Application:

The question we need to answer ourselves is:

- **"How kind am I in my responses, both in gesture, action and words?",**
- **"Is the kindness I intend to show visible and observable by others, especially those to whom I intend to show and express kindness to?"**

Make it a prepositioned intention to be kind and to pursue acts of kindness every day. The most recognizable international sign of Kindness is said to be that of an endearing and warm-hearted smile. Practice your smile, and offer a smile to people wherever you go. Pursue opportunities to show unexpected kindness and help to people wherever you can everyday. Make it part of who you are.

Prayer:

"Father God, thank you for Your daily Kindness towards me. I pray that I will be kind like You are. Your Care, considerate and kind-hearted dealings with my shortcomings and failures over-

whelm me. Help me to as thoughtful and gentle with the failures of others today. May Your Kindness be seen in me I want to show Your kindness to all. I pray for Your Kindness to fill every conversation and response of my life."

WATCHFULNESS

Definition:

Watchfulness is the action and activity of paying close attention to one's own, and other's lives, especially as it impacts others positively for Christ's sake.

Scripture:

*Matthew 16:5 (NIV) "⁶ "**Be careful,**" Jesus said to them. "**Be on your guard** against the yeast of the Pharisees and Sadducees." Matthew 16:11-12*

*Mark 13:33,35 (NIV) "³³ **Be on guard! Be alert!** You do not know when that time will come. ³⁵ "Therefore **keep watch** because you do not know when the owner of the house will come back—whether in the evening, or at midnight, or when the rooster crows, or at dawn. ³⁶ If he comes suddenly, do not let him find you* *sleeping.³⁷ What I say to you, I say to everyone:* **'Watch!'**"

*Luke 12:15 (NIV) "¹⁵ Then he said to them, "***Watch out! Be on your guard*** against all kinds of greed; life does not consist in an abundance of possessions."*

Titus 2:12 "Teaching us that, denying ungodliness and worldly lusts, **we should live soberly, righteously, and godly,** *in this present world."*

Hebrews 2:1-4 (NIV) "2 **We must pay the most careful attention,** *therefore, to what we have heard, so that we do not drift away. ² For since the message spoken through angels was binding, and every violation and disobedience received its just punishment, ³ how shall we escape if we ignore so great a salvation? This salvation, which was first announced by the Lord, was confirmed to us by those who heard him. ⁴ God also testified to it by signs, wonders and various miracles, and by gifts of the Holy Spirit distributed according to his will."*

Mark 14:38 (NIV) " ³⁸ **Watch and pray** *so that you will not fall into temptation. The spirit is willing, but the flesh is weak."*

Acts 20:28 (NIV) " ²⁸ **Keep watch over yourselves** *and all the flock of which the Holy Spirit has made you overseers. Be shepherds of the church of God,[a] which he bought with his own blood."*

2 Corinthians 10:5 (NIV) "⁵ We demolish arguments and every pretension that sets itself up against the knowledge of God, and **we take captive every thought to make it obedient to Christ.***"*

Characteristic explained:

Watchfulness is the act of being alert and observant: alert as to possible dangers and endangering situations or influences, and at the same time observant over one's own example in every life situation.

Watchfulness is also defined and described by having a sense of alertness, paying attention, having a careful awareness, a mindfulness and readiness to apply oneself with keenness and vigilance.

Watchfulness requires us to make a commitment to take unruly and wayward thoughts captive. Watchfulness is also the activity of applying caution and to be on your guard.

Life Application:

A question to ask is:

- **"How alert and observant am I to observe endangering influences?**
- **How vigilant am I to set up a guard and protection over my life, and that of others, when I see endangering situations arise?"**

One of the ways to harness oneself with Watchfulness is to daily put on the armour of God. The mental and prayerful application of the armour of God, over time, guards us, and prepares us to be more alert and aware to be watchful. For us as Believers it is also the daily awareness to expectantly wait for the return of our Lord. Regardless of when the Lord Jesus returns, He should find us busy with His work and applying ourselves to the tasks He gave us to do.

Let us be watchful over our lives, as to be on guard to keep our lives pure and in right standing with God. Let us also be watchful in living such lives that will be ready to meet our Lord any time of day or night. Let us build watchfulness into our spiritual and character make up. *Be watchful!*

Prayer:

" Father in Heaven, I come to You in the Mighty Name of Jesus. Father I thank you for Your Holy Spirit who is with me and in me. Thank you for giving me Your Holy Spirit. You know all things. I pray that You will help me to be alert and watchful over my life and the lives of those entrusted to my Spiritual care. Give me a discerning and observing heart to see things before they become obstacles or hurts in my life and in the lives of those under my care. Help me to be alert and to be wise in not exposing myself to unhealthy environments, conversations, engagements, friendships that might numb my sensitivity for sound judgement and staying in a right relationship with You. Give me a watchful heart, mind and spirit. Open my eyes to see, my heart to understand and my mind to perceive what You want me to do and what You want to teach me daily. May I be watchful to do what You asked me to say and do, and watchful over my words, thoughts and attitudes, that they may honor You. "

PERSEVERANCE

Definition:

Perseverance is the inbred ability to endure through difficult and hard times. It is the continuing in the faith regardless of what challenges might be encountered.

Scripture:

Galatians 6:9 "And **let us not be weary** *in well doing: for in due season we shall reap, if we faint not.*"

Hebrews 12:1 (NIV) "*[12] Therefore, since we are surrounded by such a great cloud of witnesses, let us throw off everything that hinders and the sin that so easily entangles. And* **let us run with perseverance** *the race marked out for us,*"

Romans 8:25 (NIV) "*²⁵ But if we hope for what we do not yet have,* **we wait for it patiently.**"

James 1:2-4, 12 (NIV) "*² Consider it pure joy, my brothers and sisters, whenever you face trials of many kinds, ³ because you know that* **the testing of your faith produces perseverance.** *⁴ Let perseverance finish its work so that you may be mature and complete, not lacking anything. ¹²* **Blessed is the one who perseveres under trial** *because, having stood the test, that person will receive the crown of life that the Lord has promised to those who love him.*"

1 Timothy 4:15-16 (NIV) "*¹⁵ Be diligent in these matters; give yourself wholly to them, so that everyone may see your progress. ¹⁶ Watch your life and doctrine closely.* **Persevere in them,** *because if you do, you will save both yourself and your hearers.*"

Hebrews 10:36 (NIV) "*³⁶* **You need to persevere so that** *when you have done the will of God,* **you will receive what he has promised.***" Hebrews 10:16-36.*

Characteristic explained:

Perseverance is the determined heart attitude to endure, presses on, and persist in whatever difficult situation one might find yourself in. Perseverance requires drive, insistent determination, grit, persistence and sometimes-even stubbornness to not give up or to let go of what you stand for or believe in.

. . .

PERSEVERANCE IS CLOSELY CONNECTED to our ability to endure through challenging and testing situations. Perseverance is also connected to our ability to take our stand for what we believe in regardless of the attacks that might be launched against us.

One of the outstanding values that Believers in Christ exhibit is their ability to stay the course regardless of the sometimes challenging and unfavourable circumstances they encounter or face.

Life Application:

The question we need to ask ourselves is:

- *"How strong am I standing in my faith?"*
- *"What am I prepared to do to not give up?"*

Perseverance is making a pre-determined decision that you will do whatever it takes to defend your faith. Perseverance is taking a strong and firm stand for your values. Perseverance is applying faith and hope to everyday challenges. Believers persevere so that they might receive their promised reward. Think of a challenging situation you are in or are facing at the moment where you think it is impossible to have a suitable outcome or breakthrough, well, since your faith is tested, decide to not give up hope that what God promised in His Word, will come to pass.

Prayer:

"Father God, I come to You in the Mighty Name of Jesus. Father, I pray for an enduring and a persevering heart. I need You to strengthen me and may the encouragement of Your Word carry me through every trying time in my life. Help me to remember that the trial I face help me to develop perseverance. Thank you for

giving me a spirit to endure. I trust and rely on Your strength every day. Jesus thank you for Your example of persevering through the opposition, persecution and attacks of the evil one. You stood Your ground in the midst of severe suffering. Help me to do the same. Amen"

HONOURING

Definition:

To show honour is to be respectful in gesture, words and behaviour. Being respectful is to show honour, reverence and deference to those you honour.

Scripture:

*John 5:23 (NIV) "23 **that all may honor the Son just as they honor the Father.** Whoever does not honor the Son does not honor the Father, who sent him."*

*Matthew 15:4 (NIV) "⁴ For God said, '**Honor your father and mother**' and 'Anyone who curses their father or mother is to be put to death.'*

Romans 13:7 (NIV) "*⁷ **Give to everyone what you owe them**: If you owe taxes, pay taxes; if revenue, then revenue; **if respect, then respect; if honor, then honor.**" Romans 13:1-7*

1 Timothy 6:1 (NIV) "*6 **All who are under the yoke of slavery should consider their masters worthy of full respect**, so that God's name and our teaching may not be slandered."*

1 Peter 2:17 (NIV) "*¹⁷ **Show proper respect to everyone**, love the family of believers, fear God, **honor the emperor.**"*

Leviticus 19:32 (NIV) "*³² "'**Stand up in the presence of the aged, show respect for the elderly** and revere your God. I am the Lord.*

1 Thessalonians 5:12-13 (NIV) "*2 Now we ask you, brothers and sisters, to **acknowledge those who work hard among you, who care for you in the Lord** and who admonish you. 13 **Hold them in the highest regard in love because of their work.** Live in peace with each other."*

Ephesians 6:1-3 (NIV) "*6 Children, obey your parents in the Lord, for this is right. ² "**Honor your father and mother**"—which is the first commandment with a promise— ³ "so that it may go well with you and that you may enjoy long life on the earth."*

Proverbs 3:9 (NIV) "*⁹ **Honor the Lord with your wealth, with the firstfruits of all your crops;***

> *¹⁰ then your barns will be filled to overflowing, and your vats will brim over with new wine."*
>
> *Isaiah 29:13 (NIV) "¹³ The Lord says:* ***"These people come near to me with their mouth and honor me with their lips,*** *but their hearts are far from me."*

Characteristic explained:

*WE HONOUR **when we show respect.*** Respect could be shown to God, His Words, His Servants, Elderly people, our Parents, people in official Governmental Positions, Teachers and also those earthly things entrusted to us.

We honour when we submit, respect and show admiration to people or even things. Embracing this Kingdom value means that we show respect for God when we look after everything we have, since we see them as gifts and privileges from God.

We honour when we give credit, pay tribute and show admiration. We honour when we act on principle, and present ourselves with nobility and take pride in where we live and how we conduct ourselves with others. The fact is that all of us love to have people in our lives that take pride in what we do or what we accomplished. In this way we feel honoured.

We honour when we treat people as if it is a privilege for us to be associated with them, and have the pleasure of their company.

Life Application:

We honour God when we credit Him for all He does in our lives. ***Honour God!*** Honour God, not just with our lips, but from our hearts. One of the ways in which we honour God is by returning to Him a tenth of all our income. Honour

God by Tithing! We value honouring God when we uphold the Leaders of the Country we live in, up in our prayers and submit to their authority. Honour God by honouring the Leader in Government! Honour Governmental Leaders! Honour those who are over you in the Lord. Show them the highest respect, because of the Lord. Honour your Spiritual Leaders! Honour one another by being respectful. Be Respectful! Honour always brings you into the presence of those in high authority and Leadership. Keep along the pathways of honour and it will put you in good standing with those who high places. Never become too familiar!

Prayer:

"Heavenly Father, I honor You as my Father, my Great Shepherd, my God and Master. You are my Creator. You are Kind, Compassionate, Caring and Merciful. You are Forgiving and Gracious. I love You and Worship at Your feet today. I come on bended knees and a humble heart before You. May I honor You in my thoughts, my words and my actions. May I bring honor to You through the way I live and behave. You are central and take preeminence in my life. I honor You for my Father and Mother. I thank you for them and the faith they instilled in me as a young child. I pray for the Leader and Leadership of the Governing Authorities in my Nation. I pray that they will all be saved and be good instruments in Your hands to govern us well. I pray and honor You for the Spiritual Leaders in my life. I pray for their protection, good health and good fortune. I honor You! Amen!"

SUBMISSIVE

Definition:

*S*ubmission is the self-determined subjection to the will of another. For us as Believers it is primarily to submit ourselves, through thought, words and actions, to the Will and Word of God.

Scripture:

*Hebrews 5:7-9 (NIV) "⁷ During the days of Jesus' life on earth, he offered up prayers and petitions with fervent cries and tears to the one who could save him from death, and **he was heard because of his reverent submission.** ⁸ Son though he was, he learned obedience from what he suffered ⁹ and, once made perfect, he became the source of eternal salvation for all who obey him."*

Hebrews 13:17 (NIV) "*Obey them that have the rule over you, and* **submit yourselves:** *for they watch for your souls, as they that must give account, that they may do it with joy, and not with grief: for that is unprofitable for you.*"

Romans 13:1 (NIV) "*13* **Let everyone be subject to the governing authorities***, for there is no authority except that which God has established. The authorities that exist have been established by God.*"

Romans 13:5 (NIV) "*⁵ Therefore, it* **is necessary to submit to the authorities***, not only because of possible punishment but also as a matter of conscience.*"

James 4:7 (NIV) "*⁷* **Submit yourselves, then, to God.** *Resist the devil, and he will flee from you.*"

James 4:9 (NIV) "*¹⁰* **Humble yourselves before the Lord***, and he will lift you up.*"

Proverbs 3:5-6 (NIV) "*⁵ Trust in the Lord with all your heart and lean not on your own understanding; ⁶* **in all your ways submit to him***, and he will make your paths straight.*"

1 Peter 5:5-6 (NIV) "*⁵ In the same way, you who are younger,* **submit yourselves to your elders. All of you, clothe yourselves with humility toward one another***, because, "***God opposes the proud, but shows favor to the humble.***" ⁶* **Humble yourselves, therefore, under God's mighty hand***, that he may lift you up in due time.*"

Characteristic explained:

For us as Believers, *Submission is to subject oneself to the God, His Son, His Word, His Will, His Holy Spirit, His Leaders and His Guidance.*

To submit requires humility, obedience, compliance and willing following. Submission and Obedience could almost be used interchangeably within the context of the Kingdom of God Value System. It requires obedience to submit, and submission to obey everything the Lord taught us. There also exist a close relationship with the Value of Humility in Submission and Obedience.

Submission requires us to consider the Will of God over that of ours. Submission requires adherence to the Bible, the Holy Spirit as well as those whom God placed over us in the Church.

Life Application:

The question is:

- *"How submitted am I to the Will of God?"*

One way of developing this Value of Submission in our lives is of course to pray and meditate on it, especially when we pray the *"Our Father"* prayer. Jesus taught us in the "Our Father" prayer to pray: *"May Your Will be done, on earth as it is in Heaven"*. We can't ask God to let His Will be done on earth, without it including us, and in our lives. Submission starts with submitting to the Will and Purpose of God in our lives.

No submission is truly possible if it is not rooted in our humble submission to the Will and Purposes of God, however, if we truly submit ourselves to God, then all other requirements for submission will not be seen as unrealistic and legalistic Christian laws, but something we want to honour because of our love for the Lord.

Pray for the Government of your nation. Pray for the Leaders God placed over you, at work, at school, and at your Church, and as you pray for them, also pledge your allegiance to their authority over you.

I wonder what impact it would have on the governments of the world if we, His people, will start to earnestly praying for our leaders? I am sure our nations will be healed and restored. One person can make a difference. I pray that you will start, where you are, and submit, and become an example of someone who lives in submission to the Will and Purpose of God.

Prayer:

"Heavenly Father, I humbly bow before You today, not just in action but also in heart, attitude and mind. I submit myself to Your authority, Your Word and Will. I know that no submission to anyone or anything else is possible without a heartfelt submission to You first. I therefor submit myself to Your Will. May Your Will be done in my life as You've determined it in Heaven. I want Your Will to be done in my marriage, my family, my business, my ministry and in every activity of my life. May the life a life and lead show my absolute surrender and submission to You. Amen!"

AFTERWORD

In conclusion on Values.

I found and determined many more Values throughout Scripture, however narrowed the values down to 52 Kingdom Values so that we can revisited them over the course of the 52 weeks of a year. Through this humble submission, I have outlined and explored these for adoption and application in our lives.

There are many Biblical truths that we value. I pray that we will be the generation to make fresh pursuits to pursue godliness out of a pure heart. I pray that we will be those who train ourselves to be godly, under the directive of the Holy Spirit.

The Holy Spirit is indispensable in the process of Sanctification

The Holy Spirit is indispensable in this process of sanctification, and of course the **Fruit of the Spirit are Spiritual Values** by which we are often characterized and determined to be Children of God, however, these come as a ***direct result of the Holy Spirit's presence and pre-eminence*** in our lives.

> *Galatians 5:22-23 (GNB)* "*²² But* **when the Holy Spirit controls our lives he will produce this kind of fruit in us**: *love, joy, peace, patience, kindness, goodness, faithfulness, ²³ gentleness and self-control; and here there is no conflict with Jewish laws.*"

Last but not least

Love – the greatest value of all.

The greatest Value that sets us apart as Disciples of the Lord is of course Love.

> *"By this shall all men know that you are My Disciples, if you have love one for another."*

These words, and many more, from the teachings of Jesus to His Disciples, and us, stand out as Lighthouses in our journey to assimilate the Values of the Kingdom of God. Our part is to live the values.

Assimilating the Values of the Kingdom of God is one thing, however, maintaining them in our lives is another, and **it is** therefor **equally important to establish spiritual disciplines**, which will ensure that these Values are kept and maintained.

Our Character is forged along the pathway of living intentionally disciplined spiritual lives in alignment within the guidelines of the Bible.

NOTES

INTRODUCTION

1. Wilson Todd, Dream Big, pg. 29, iBooks
2. Wilson Todd, Dream Big, pg. 29, iBooks
3. Ralph W. Neighbour Jr., Life Basic Training, back page, Touch Publications

2. VALUES DEFINED

1. Businessdictionary.com
2. Wikipedia.com
3. *An Intermediate Greek-English Lexicon.* 1889.
4. Kidder, Rushworth (2003). *How Good People Make Tough Choices: Resolving the Dilemmas of Ethical Living.* New York: Harper Collins. p. 63. ISBN 0-688-17590-2.
5. Paul, Richard; Elder, Linda (2006). *The Miniature Guide to Understanding the Foundations of Ethical Reasoning.* United States: Foundation for Critical Thinking Free Press. p. NP. ISBN 0-944583-17-2.
6. John Deigh in Robert Audi (ed), *The Cambridge Dictionary of Philosophy,* 1995.
7. Paul, Richard; Elder, Linda (2006). *The Miniature Guide to Understanding the Foundations of Ethical Reasoning.* United States: Foundation for Critical Thinking Free Press. p. np. ISBN 0-944583-17-2.
8. Catechism of Roman Catholic Church,
9. Wikipedia.com
10. Collinsdictionary.com
11. Wikipedia.com
12. Wikipedia.com
13. Merriam-webster.com

Made in the USA
Columbia, SC
20 April 2025